NOW IS BETTER

Stefan Sagmeister

Foreword: Beautiful Numbers Steven Pinker

Can numbers be beautiful? Can they be noble, moral, uplifting, inspiring, sublime? For many centuries, mystics and rationalists alike have believed them to be all of these things. The Pythagoreans of the sixth century BCE believed that "beatitude is the knowledge of the perfection of the numbers of the soul," or, more pithily, "All is number." The Jewish cabalists sought hidden meanings in the sums of the ranks of the letters making up a word. The Galilean revolution in science was propelled by his credo that "the book of nature is written in the language

◀ WOMAN II

Percentage of countries with
at least one female member
of parliament, 1920–2020

of mathematics." Some physicists today, noting that their own theories are nothing but equations and have no need to stipulate that "stuff exists," speculate that the universe itself consists of mathematical entities, sometimes called "it from bit."

But the beauty of numbers need not reside only in the pristine symmetries and regularities of the abstract numbers themselves. Numbers can represent things in the world—they can be *data*. And data, too, can be beautiful.

An unsung hero of humanity is John Graunt, a seventeenth-century British haberdasher who studied mortality reports as a hobby and thereby invented epidemiology. In the centuries since, knowledge of how many people live and how many die under which circumstances has distinguished dangerous superstition from lifesaving public health and medicine, multiplying our life spans and saving children by the billions.

But numbers in the form of data are tragically underappreciated by

MURDER ▶

Homicides in Europe per 100,000 people, 1400–2000

our journalistic and artistic elites. "Data" has become a scary word, a resource exploited by tech companies to steal our privacy and our attention.

Yet data, mobilized for the good of humankind, is a vital moral force, a bulwark against the primitive fallacies and biases built into our brains. Among the most robust findings in cognitive science is the availability heuristic: people judge probability by how easily they can bring anecdotes and images and narratives to mind. Since actual probability consists of the number of occurrences as a proportion of the number of opportunities, regardless of how salient or memorable or viral they may be, we can't count on our intuitions to reflect reality.

Worse still, the nature of journalism combines with our availability bias to guarantee that "well-informed" readers will be systematically deluded about the state of the world and which way it's going. The news is a nonrandom sample of the worst things happening on Earth at any moment, a collection of lurid anecdotes and images and narratives. Since there are so many more ways for things to go wrong than right, most of these episodes will be terrible. Things that go right are often nonevents—a city not attacked by terrorists, a country free from famine or infectious disease—or gradual trends that creep up by a few percentage points a year, compounding to transform the world by stealth. Surveys confirm that people's understanding of world trends is wildly out of touch with reality, almost always toward the downside.[1]

Numbers, in the form of data that captures the true state of the world and how it has changed, are a precious corrective to these delusions. And an awareness of the numbers does more than just help us on a current-events quiz: it steers our convictions toward those that are truly moral. It makes us aware that improvements in the human condition are feasible, not utopian or romantic or idealistic, and thereby emboldens us to work for more of them. It counters the cynicism and fatalism that justify enjoying oneself while one can since there's nothing to be done. And it counters the radicalism that commends burning it all down in the dangerous hope that anything that rises out of the rubble will be better than what we have now.

And it is numbers that truly implement the ideal that "all people are created equal." Our unguided empathy is diverted by superficialities that have nothing to do with moral worth—how similar a person is to us, how close in space, how photogenic. Numbers abstract away from these irrelevancies and, paradoxically, represent real people, each a locus of suffering and flourishing. "A million lives saved" means someone like you, and your mother, and your child, and your lover, and your best friend . . . continue this thought a million times.

We are beginning to see an aesthetic appreciation of data, commensurate with its moral value, in elegant infographics like the website Information Is Beautiful. Beautiful, yes, but hardly art. The creations of Stefan Sagmeister, inspired by the same respect for numbers,

WOMAN I ▶

Percentage of countries in which women have the right to vote, 1900–2000

are altogether different. They start from a deep appreciation of the legacy of Western artistic motifs, adding visual anomalies that at first challenge and surprise and puzzle their viewers before giving way to an epiphany that informs and delights. They have created an entirely new way in which numbers can be inspiring, amusing, edifying, and, yes, beautiful.

◄ LITERACY I

Percentage of people who can
read and write, 1900–2000

1   See, for example, Hans and Ola Rosling's
    Ignorance Project: www.gapminder.org/ignorance.

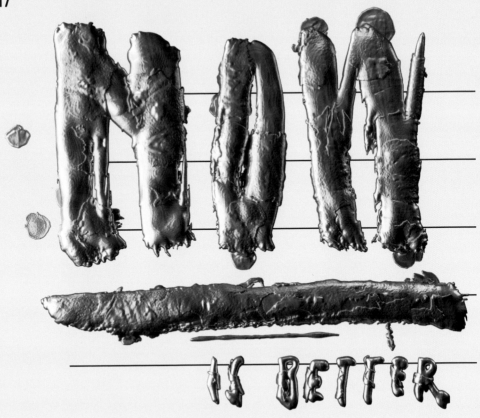

I have observed that not the man who hopes when others despair, but the man who despairs when others hope, is admired by a large class of persons as a sage. — John Stuart Mill

NOW IS BETTER. Most of us prefer life over death, food over hunger, health over sickness, and peace over war. We'd rather live in democracies than in dictatorships, we'd rather be knowledgeable than ignorant.

All of these things can be measured. And over the past two hundred years, all of these things *have been* measured! We have excellent data from authoritative sources. And all of them have gotten better.

When I look at long-term human development, most aspects of our lives have improved significantly. Fewer people go hungry, fewer people die in wars or as a result of natural disasters, and more people than

◀ **HER MARK**

Universal voting rights for women, 1916–2017

ever before live in democracies—living much longer lives. Two hundred years ago, nine out of ten people could neither read nor write, now it is just one out of ten.[1]

Many things do go right, though the media has told us the exact opposite for years. At the time of publication, we continue to recover from a global pandemic, monkeypox lurks around the corner, war rages in Europe, and many countries are suffering the effects of worsening climate change. We have a better chance of finding a solution for these problems from a position of acknowledging past successes than from a place of doom and gloom.

I am a designer. Exploring complex subjects, selecting the essential strands, and transforming them into something that can be understood by a large audience defines what I do.

I will try.

RICHER AND POORER ▶

Top row of triangles: Percentage of the global population living in poverty, 1990–2020
Bottom row of triangles: Results of a 2020 survey in which people shared their thoughts on the global poverty rate in the last thirty years

1 Max Roser and Esteban Ortiz-Ospina, "Literacy," *Our World in Data*, August 13, 2016, www.ourworldindata.org/literacy.

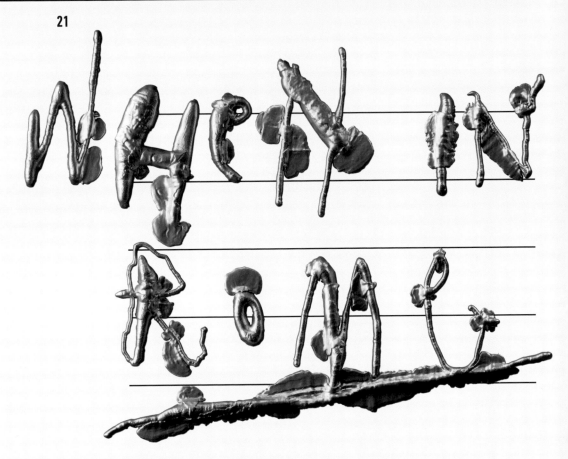

WHEN IN ROME. The American Academy in Rome is housed in a grand villa near the peak of the famous Gianicolo Hill, overlooking the Trastevere neighborhood and the city of Rome beyond. As a designer in residence there, I was provided a beautiful apartment and studio for three months, where a little sign informed visitors that this particular workspace had been funded by Mr. and Mrs. David Rockefeller.[1]

Besides the unparalleled research library, containing an abundance of rare art and architecture books, the most thrilling feature of the academy was its excellent food program. Created by farm-to-table innovator Alice Waters, the Rome Sustainable Food Project drew most of the seventy-odd Rome Prize fellows and resident artists away from their studies for lunch and dinner. The ever-changing seating order in

the academy's gorgeous dining room encouraged dialogues between archaeologists, artists, writers, musicians, architects, and designers in what felt like a twice-daily salon.

One evening, I was seated next to the husband of one of the invited artists. During the course of our conversation, I learned he was a lawyer, and he informed me that we are witnessing the end of modern democracy in some places—citing Poland, Hungary, and Brazil—as extreme right-wing governments are being elected around the world. After dinner, I returned to my studio to investigate.

When did modern democracy start? How did it develop?

A quick online search revealed that more than two hundred years ago, only one democracy existed: the United States. One hundred years later, right after World War I, there were nineteen democratic countries. Today, 96 out of 167 countries are largely considered to be democratic. For the first time in human history, more than half of the global population lives in a democratic system.[2]

Upon learning this, I realized my dinner companion could not have been more wrong. This highly intelligent lawyer did not understand the reality of the world he lives in.

As a communication designer, this opened a promising line of thinking.

1   I was a resident there from May to July 2019.
2   Bastian Herre and Max Roser, "Democracy,"
    Our World in Data, March 15, 2013,
    www.ourworldindata.org/democracy.

DEMOCRACY II

Number of democracies vs.
autocracies worldwide,
1920 vs. 2020

Life is better

We choose food

Knowledge beats

We prefer health

Democracy over

Peace

than death.

over hunger.

ignorance.

over sickness.

dictatorships.

over war.

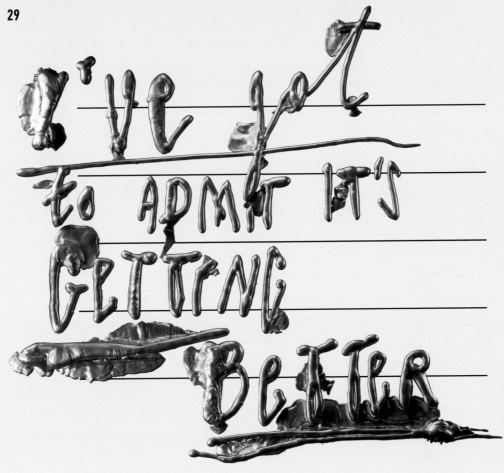

I'VE GOT TO ADMIT, IT'S GETTING BETTER.[1] Throughout the ages, we have come up with a number of ways to help improve our personal lives, our communities, and our world. These include human rights, nonviolence, and working together. We have developed institutions around the societal pillars of science, education, media, and democracy.[2]

Most of us would rather be alive than dead.

◀ STAYING ALIVE

Life expectancy in Austria, the United States, and the United Kingdom over various periods of time, pending when data was available, 1550–2014

We now enjoy more than double the amount of time on this Earth than our ancestors did only two centuries ago.[3] This is progress. And this advancement happened not just in wealthy countries, but in the poorer ones as well: between 2003 and 2013, the average life expectancy in Kenya increased by a full ten years. So if you lived in Kenya during those years, you paradoxically did not get older—after ten years, death did not come any closer.[4] And a century ago, half a million people used to die as a result of natural disasters every year, which has now been reduced to a tenth of that number. This is even more remarkable when you consider there are four times as many people living today.[5]

Our workplaces have become safer: accidental deaths while on the job are down 90 percent from one hundred years ago.

And our workplaces have become safer: accidental deaths while on the job are down 90 percent from one hundred years ago. And, incredibly, walking around our cities is also now much safer, as compared to when people still traveled by horse-drawn buggy.[6]

We prefer food over hunger.

Growing up in Austria, one of the most popular fairy tales centered on a mythical place called the Schlaraffenland, a land in which golden pancakes grow on trees and roasted pigs walk around with forks in their backs. I now experience a version of that Schlaraffenland every day in New York City, where those golden pancakes and roasted pigs are just a call away.

The energy value of a typical diet in eighteenth-century France was similar to the energy value of a typical diet in Rwanda in 1965, which was then the single most malnourished country in the world.[7] Since the 1800s, the percentage of people living in extreme poverty has fallen from 90 percent to less than 10 percent. The United Nations now predicts we will see the end of extreme poverty within our lifetimes.[8]

We favor health over sickness.

How does COVID-19 compare to other pandemics of the past two hundred years?

Since the early 1980s, thirty million have succumbed to HIV/AIDS. In the beginning of the twentieth century, the Spanish flu killed fifty million people. Throughout the nineteenth century, twelve million died of the plague. Seven million have died from COVID-19 at the time of this publication.[9]

If we imagine the isolated squalor that survivors of the Spanish flu must have lived in—very few had running water, radios, telephones, or television—we can safely assume they were not complaining about the plethora of Zoom calls and the scarcity of shows on Netflix. Today, nearly every person in the United States enjoys running water, and more people throughout the world are getting their water from a protected source than ever before.[10]

Like the Spanish flu, smallpox was similarly devastating, existing for more than three thousand years unchecked and killing more than three hundred million people in the twentieth century alone. As a result of a global vaccination effort, it has ceased to exist.[11] While vaccinations were still rare in the nineteenth century, 86 percent of all children worldwide are vaccinated against tetanus today.[12]

We'd rather be more equal.

Countries ranking at the top of the annual worldwide happiness index tend to show high levels of equality, as measured with

the Gini index. A Gini index of 1 means that everything is owned by a single person, while a Gini index of 0 indicates that everyone owns the same amount. The lower the score, the more equal the society.

We've all been reading about how we are living in a time of great inequality. This proves to be true if you only look at the past fifty years, exclusively observing resource-rich countries. In the past five decades, the Gini index in the United States has gone from 0.44 to 0.51, as fewer people claim ownership over the sum possessions of the country compared to fifty years ago.[13]

And yet, it is worth noting that this inequity existed well beyond fifty years ago, and was significantly worse before then. The adjusted net worth of the Vanderbilts or the Rockefellers is substantially higher when compared to the net worths of the Elon Musks and Jeff Bezoses of today. Scholars estimate John D. Rockefeller to have been about three times as rich as Bezos.[14] More significantly, disenfranchised men and women in nineteenth-century America were much poorer than the contemporary version of this socioeconomic class today. Two hundred years ago, 90 percent of the global population lived in abject poverty and were ruled over by a tiny elite.

Considering gender equality, the share of women in the top income groups has only improved from 20 percent to 28 percent over the past few decades, and there are still more gains to be made.[15] However, thirty years ago, half of the US population believed women should remain in the kitchen. A quarter of the country shares this belief today.[16] Thankfully, female representation in government has increased significantly.[17] If you ever get the opportunity to use a time machine, it would be smart to elect going forward into the future rather than back into the past (unless you're John D. Rockefeller).

◄ SPIKES

Percentage of children vaccinated against diphtheria, whooping cough, and tetanus, 1880–2020

Knowledge and strength beat ignorance and weakness.

In 1800, only 12 percent of the global population could read and write. Now, more than three-quarters of the worldwide population is literate.[18] Consequently, more books are published now than ever before.

Because we know more, we also play more. For example, there were only two hundred playable guitars available per one million people in the 1960s. This number increased to eleven thousand guitars per one million people today.[19]

We also exercise more. The first New York City Marathon took place in 1970—of the one hundred and twenty-seven people who took part, fifty-five finished. The *New York Times* estimates that about two hundred Americans were in good enough shape to finish a marathon in 1970. Today, one needs to take part in a lottery to be granted the opportunity to be one of the fifty thousand people to participate in the race.[20]

We'd rather live in peace than in war.

Throughout most of human history, peace was defined as an interlude in between wars. Such conflict between the great powers represented the most intense forms of destruction and were responsible for the most misery.[21] But these great powers are no longer at war with one another: the last conflict pitted the United States against Korea over sixty years ago. As Steven Pinker points out in his book *Enlightenment Now*, the idea that it is inherently honorable to kill people and destroy their bridges, farms, and schools strikes most people

STARA BIEDA ▶

Worldwide poverty rate, 1920–2020

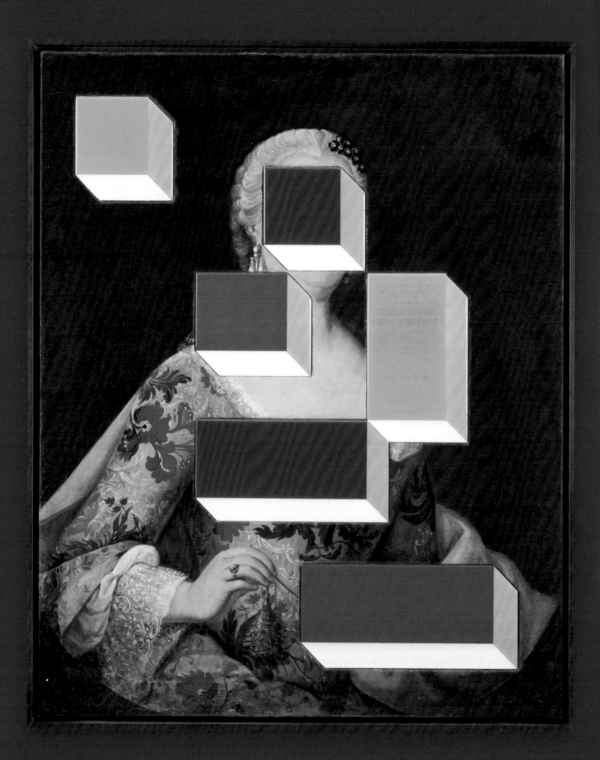

today as completely crazy. A century ago, this thought was common not only among the military but also among many artists and intellectuals. Émile Zola wrote that "war is life itself."[22] John Ruskin called war "the foundation of all arts."[23]

In contrast, the war raging in the Ukraine at the time of publication draws almost universal condemnation. No one believes the Russian aggression to be part of life itself. And yet the idea that global conflict used to be even more devastating than today offers little solace to people under attack by Russian bombs.

Throughout most of human history, peace was defined as an interlude in between wars.

Progress will never be steady. As Pinker writes: "...solutions to problems create new problems. But progress can resume when the new problems are solved in their turn."[24]

For those who are living in countries at peace, the number of homicides committed globally has been consistently on the decline since the 1400s, dwindling from thirty-five murders per one hundred thousand people all the way down to two per one hundred thousand. In other words, you were almost twenty times more likely to be killed at the hands of another in the Middle Ages than you are today.[25]

We'd rather live in democracies than in dictatorships.

When I grew up in Europe, countries like Spain and Portugal were governed by fascist regimes. Poland, Czechoslovakia, Romania, Bulgaria, and most other countries in Eastern Europe were ruled autocratically. For the first time in human history, more than half of the world's population lives in a democracy.[26] This is a fantastic

◀ JOSEFINE

Percentage of women working in the United States over one hundred years, 1910–2010 achievement, as democracies enjoy higher rates of economic growth, fewer wars and genocides, as well as healthier and better-educated citizens.[27]

One of the most impressive data sets I've ever come across compared the duration and intensity of famines by political regimes over the past two hundred years: almost all historic famines took place in autocratic countries under ruthless regimes, with very few occurring in a democratic system.[28]

The environment is not totally fucked.

When I arrived in New York City thirty-five years ago, it would have been unthinkable to consider eating a fish captured in the Hudson River. While I'd still likely prefer something else on the menu, there's a good chance we will be able to enjoy locally caught fish from the city's surrounding waterways again soon.[29]

In the summer months of the 1950s and 1960s, the city was under a near-permanent cover of smog when heat inversions trapped particles from chimneys and vehicles nearer to the ground. This became so bad that airports were temporarily shut down and hundreds of people died as a result of respiratory illness.[30]

Today when I walk the streets of New York in the middle of August, my nose picks up the smell of pizza, subway odors, sugar maple trees, traces of donuts, whiffs of garbage, and dog shit, all topped off by the strong stench of marijuana. The smog from cars and chimneys doesn't cut through. The fact that New York was able to manage its air pollution might serve

WAR! WAR! ▶

Percentage of years in which the great powers have fought one another for an extended period (at least twenty-five years), 1500–2000

JOHANNA

Global child mortality rate, 1800 vs. 2020

DANGEROUS PEOPLE

Number of murders committed
by female killers vs. male killers
in the United States, 2020

as an example for the many cities around the world where smog is still a problem.

While we read about large catastrophes in our oceans, like the Exxon Valdez or BP Deepwater Horizon oil spills, we know very little about the slow and steady improvements being made overall in this industry each year.[31]

Sustainable environmental progress is not anecdotal—it is measured by the Environmental Performance Index (EPI), a system which takes the quality of air, water, forests, farms, and natural habitats into account. Out of the 180 countries that have been tracked over the past decade, all but two EPIs have improved.[32] Wealthy countries, like those in northern Europe, improved the most, while Afghanistan and some sub-Saharan countries lagged behind.

Leaf blowers and other small gas-powered gardening equipment create roughly the same amount of ozone pollution as all of the passenger cars in California combined.

On a smaller, though shockingly large, scale: leaf blowers and other small gas-powered gardening equipment create roughly the same amount of ozone pollution as all of the passenger cars in California combined. As of 2024, the sale of gas-powered landscaping equipment will be outlawed in California.[33]

If I had a hammer.

Progress in technology lets us do more with less. A single smartphone replaces countless consumer products: a telephone, answering machine, book, camera, tape recorder, radio, alarm clock, calculator, Rolodex, dictionary, calendar, street map, flashlight, and compass, among others. We have passed a peak in our consumption of stuff: in the UK, the average person consumed fifteen tons of material every year in 2001. By 2013, this has been reduced to ten tons.[34]

The number of hours we spend doing housework, which for many counts among one's least-favorite use of time, fell from fifty-eight hours per week in 1900 to fifteen in 2010.[35] Electricity, running water, the washing machine, and the refrigerator have significantly increased the number of hours we get to spend as we wish.

In other words, the data reveals that John Lennon and Paul McCartney got it exactly right when they wrote: "I have to admit, it's getting better."

1   John Lennon and Paul McCartney, "Getting Better," track 4 on *Sgt. Pepper's Lonely Hearts Club Band*, Capitol, 1967.

2   Steven Pinker, *Enlightenment Now: The Case for Reason, Science, Humanism, and Progress* (New York: Viking, 2018), 28.

3   Max Roser, Esteban Ortiz-Ospina, and Hannah Ritchie, "Life Expectancy," *Our World in Data*, May 23, 2013, www.ourworldindata.org/life-expectancy.

4   Johan Norberg, *Progress: Ten Reasons to Look Forward to the Future* (London: Oneworld, 2018), 40–46.

5   Hannah Ritchie and Max Roser, "Natural Disasters," *Our World in Data*, 2021, www.ourworldindata.org/natural-disasters.

6   National Highway Traffic Safety Administration and National Center for Statistics and Analysis.

7   Robert William Fogel, *The Escape from Hunger and Premature Death, 1700–2100: Europe, America, and the Third World* (Cambridge, UK: University Press, 2004), 8.

8   Pinker, *Enlightenment Now*, 322.

9   "Why the HIV Epidemic Is Not Over," *World Health Organization*, 2022, www.who.int/news-room/spotlight/why-the-hiv-epidemic-is-not-over; "1918 Pandemic (H1N1 Virus)," *CDC*, June 16, 2020, www.cdc.gov/flu/pandemic-resources/1918-pandemic-h1n1.html; Kara Rogers, "Plague: History," *Encyclopedia Britannica*, 2019, www.britannica.com/science/plague/History; Hannah Ritchie, Esteban Ortiz-Ospina, Max Roser et al., "Coronavirus (COVID-19) Deaths," *Our World in Data*, 2022, www.ourworldindata.org/covid-deaths.

10 Hannah Ritchie and Max Roser, "Clean Water," *Our World in Data*, 2021, www.ourworldindata.org/water-access.

11 Sophie Ochmann and Max Roser, "Smallpox," *Our World in Data*, 2018, www.ourworldindata.org/smallpox.

12 "Immunization Coverage," *World Health Organization*, July 15, 2021, www.who.int/news-room/fact-sheets/detail/immunization-coverage.

13 Branko Milanovic, "Global Inequality by the Numbers: In History and Now," *World Bank Development Research Group*, November 1, 2012, www.documents.worldbank.org/curated/en/959251468176687085/Global-income-inequality-by-the-numbers-in-history-and-now-an-overview.

14 "The Wealthiest Historical Figures and How Much They Would Be Worth in Today's Dollars," *TitleMax*, January 30, 2019, www.titlemax.com/discovery-center/money-finance/wealthiest-historical-figures-in-todays-dollars.

15 Anthony Atkinson, Alessandra Casarico, and Sarah Voitchovsky, "Top Incomes and the Gender Divide," *Journal of Economic Inequality* 16, no. 2 (2018): 225–56.

16 Pew Research Center, "Chapter 2: Public Views on Changing Gender Roles," *Pew Research Center's Social & Demographic Trends Project*, May 29, 2013, www.pewresearch.org/social-trends/2013/05/29/chapter-2-public-views-on-changing-gender-roles.

17 Melanie M. Hughes and Pamela Paxton, "The Political Representation of Women over Time," *The Palgrave Handbook of Women's Political Rights*, October 26, 2018, 33–51.

18 Max Roser and Esteban Ortiz-Ospina, "Literacy," *Our World in Data*, August 13, 2016, www.ourworldindata.org/literacy.

19 Hans Rosling, *Factfulness: Ten Reasons We're Wrong About the World and Why Things Are Better Than You Think* (London: Hodder & Stoughton), 64.

20 "2022 TCS New York City Marathon to Return at Full Capacity with 50,000 Runners," *New York Road Runners*, February 4, 2022, www.nyrr.org/media-center/press-release/20220224_2022tcsnycmfieldsize.

21 A "great power" is a state that has the expertise to exercise its power globally. During various times in history, England, France, Germany, Russia, China, Korea, and the United States have been considered great powers.

22 James Joll and Gordon Martel, *The Origins of the First World War* (New York: Routledge, 2006), 153.

23 "Ruskin on War: Extract from the Sermon of Rev. F. O. Hall, Entitled, 'The Gospel According to John Ruskin,'" *The Cambridge Chronicle*, February 10, 1900, 15.

24 Pinker, *Enlightenment Now*, 44.

25 Pieter Spierenburg, *A History of Murder: Personal Violence in Europe from the Middle Ages to the Present* (Oxford: Polity, 2008), 4.

26 Monty Marshall, Ted Gurr, and Keith Jaggers, "Polity IV Project: Political Regime Characteristics and Transitions, 1800–2016," *Center for Systemic Peace*, June 25, 2017, www.systemicpeace.org/inscr/p4manualv2016.pdf.

27 Democracies have faster-growing economies. Note that this can be obscured by the fact that poor countries can grow at faster rates than rich countries, and poor countries tend to be less democratic: Steven Radelet, *The Great Surge: The Ascent of the Developing World* (New York: Simon & Schuster, 2016), 125–29. Democracies are less likely to go to war: Håvard Hegre, "Democracy and Armed Conflict," *Journal of Peace Research* 51, no. 2 (2014): 159–72, www.doi.org/10.1177/0022343313512852; Håvard Hegre, John Oneal, and Bruce Russett, "Trade Does Promote Peace," *Journal of Peace Research* 47, no. 6 (2010): 763–74, www.doi.org/10.1177/0022343310385995; Bruce Russett and John Oneal, *Triangulating Peace: Democracy, Interdependence, and International Organizations* (New York: W. W. Norton, 2001). Democracies have less severe (though not necessarily fewer) civil wars: Lars-Erik Cederman, Simon Hug, and Lutz Krebs, "Democratization and Civil War: Empirical Evidence," *Journal of Peace Research* 47, no. 4 (2010): 377–94, www.jstor.org/stable/20752195; Bethany Lacina, "Explaining the Severity of Civil Wars," *Journal of Conflict Resolution* 50, no. 2 (2006): 276–89, www.jstor.org/stable/27638487. Democracies have fewer genocides: Rudolph Rummel, "Democracy, Power, Genocide, and Mass Murder," *Journal of Conflict Resolution* 39, no. 1 (1995): 3–26, www.doi.org/10.1177/0022002795039001001; Barbara Harff, "No Lessons Learned from the Holocaust? Assessing Risks of Genocide and Political Mass Murder since 1955,"*American Political Science Review* 97, no. 1 (2003): 57–73, www.doi.org/10.1017/S0003055403000522. Democracies have fewer famines: Amartya Sen, *Development as Freedom* (Oxford: Oxford University Press, 1999); Stephen Devereux, "Famine in the Twentieth Century," *Institute of Development Studies*, no. 105 (2000), 22. Citizens in democracies are healthier: Timothy Besley and Masayuki Kudamatsu, "Health and Democracy," *American Economic Review* 96, no. 2 (April 2006): 313–18, www.doi.org/10.1257/000282806777212053. Citizens in democracies are better educated: Roser and Ortiz-Ospina, "Literacy," *Our World in Data*.

28 Joe Hasell and Max Roser, "Famines by Political Regime, 1860–2016," *Our World in Data*, December 7, 2017, www.ourworldindata.org/famines.

29 "New York State Health Advice on Eating Fish You Catch," *New York State Department of Health*, last modified May 2022, www.health.ny.gov/environmental/outdoors/fish/health_advisories.

30 Environmental Protection Agency, "Two 'Killer' Smogs the Headlines Missed," *EPA Journal* 12, no. 10 (December 1986): 27–29.

31 Max Roser and Hannah Ritchie, "Oil Spills," *Our World in Data*, 2022, www.ourworldindata.org/oil-spills.

32 "2022 EPI Results," *Environmental Performance Index*, 2022, www.epi.yale.edu/epi-results/2022/component/epi.

33 Tanya Rivera, "Gas-Powered Lawn Equipment Banned in California by 2024: Will Other States Follow?," *WFMY News 2*, December 3, 2021, www.wfmynews2.com/article/news/local/2-wants-to-know/gas-powered-lawn-equipment-banned-in-ca-by-2024-will-other-states-follow-new-equipment-sold-will-have-to-be-only-electric/83-72bca927-3e09-45e6-9965-fd76b4e3d2d6; Phil Willon, "California Moves toward Ban on Gas Lawn Mowers and Leaf Blowers," *Los Angeles Times*, October 10, 2021, www.latimes.com/california/story/2021-10-09/california-moves-toward-ban-on-gas-lawnmowers-and-leaf-blowers.

34 Pinker, *Enlightenment Now*, 135.

35 Daniel Kahneman, Alan Krueger, David Schkade, Norbert Schwarz, and Arthur Stone, "A Survey Method for Characterizing Daily Life Experience: The Day Reconstruction Method," *Science* 306, no. 5702 (2004): 1776–80; Jeremy Greenwood, Ananth Seshadri, and Mehmet Yorukoglu, "Engines of Liberation," *Review of Economic Studies* 72, no. 1 (2005): 109–33.

▲ STUFF ▶

Amount of stuff consumed yearly per person in the United Kingdom, 2000 vs. 2015

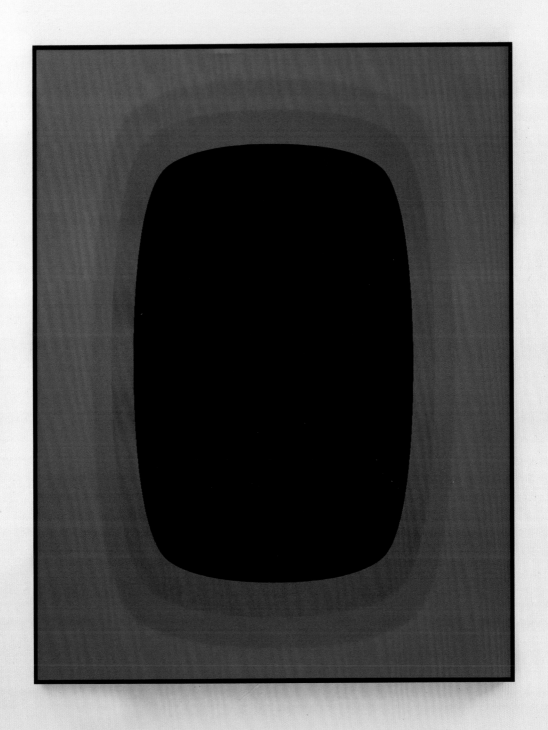

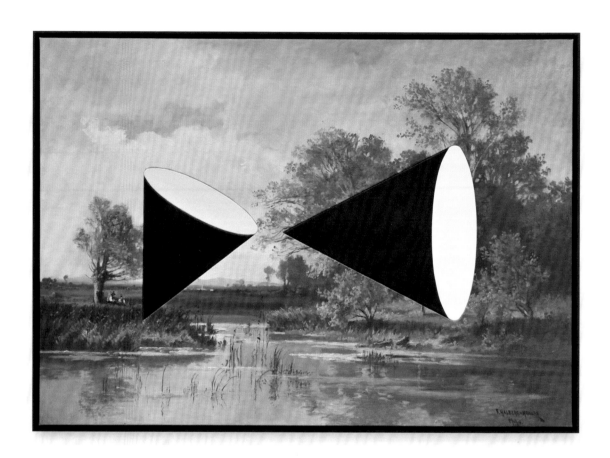

Amount of greenhouse gases
produced worldwide by
activities such as commerical
production, electricity use,
agriculture, and travel

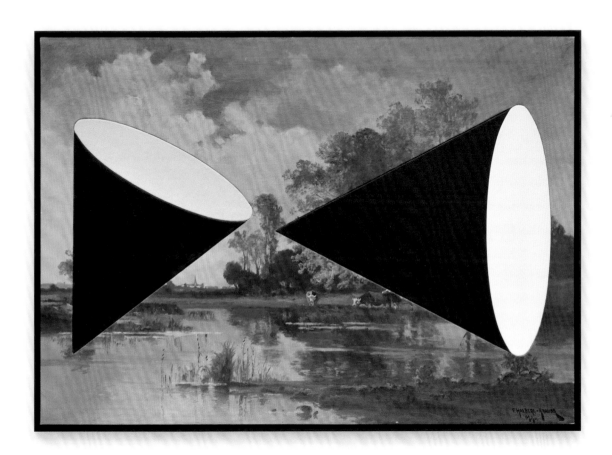

WATER

Left: Percentage of the global population with access to clean water, 1990 vs. 1998
Right: Percentage of the global population with access to clean water, 2006 vs. 2015

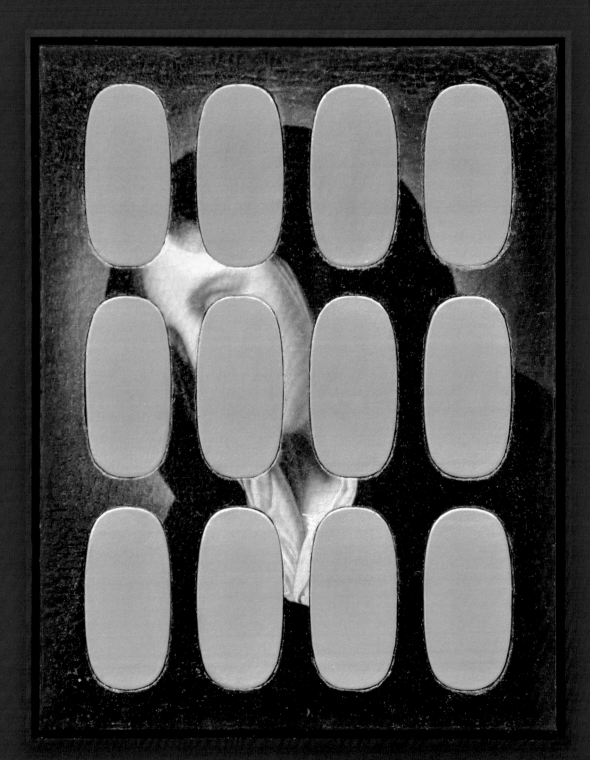

THE SAGMEISTERS OF BREGENZ. My father grew up in Bregenz, a picturesque town nestled between Lake Constance and the Austrian Alps, in the early twentieth century. The Bregenzerwald Valley reaches deep into the mountains toward the east, approaching the Arlberg mountains and Tyrol.

He shared stories of villagers from the Bregenzerwald, including tales of boys who made the terrible mistake of dating a girl from a neighboring village. This transgression prompted the local youth to stone the offending intruder, crippling the boy for life. While such stonings were officially forbidden, they were very much tolerated—and even encouraged— by adults: "He had it coming." During a tour of a small chapel while visiting the gorgeous churches of Vorarlberg, my sister and I struck up a conversation

◀ SUICIDE I

Yearly suicide rate in the United States per 100,000 people, 1950–2005

with the priest of Saint Nikolaus in Damüls, a church that is a stunning mix of Gothic and Baroque architecture originating in 1484. Beginning his service in 1985, the priest told us he abolished the "bastard bench," a particularly uncomfortable pew in the church upon which children born out of wedlock

My paternal great-great-grandparents, Jakob and Johanna Sagmeister

and their mothers were forced to sit. Things were not better in the past.

For parents, one the most tragic life events to possibly happen is the death of a child. My great-great-grandparents Jakob and Johanna Sagmeister, experienced such a tragedy not once or twice, but six times. In the 1850s, they suffered the loss of their infant children Anna Johanna, Karl Wilhelm, and Stephan Otto from scarlet fever. Their daughters Anna Maria and Regina both passed away from slime fever at the age of six, and their second daughter named Regina passed away when she was just eight years old. According to notes left by Johanna, the elder Regina predicted her own death: "Her last words were: 'In half an hour I shall be in heaven.' Exactly half an hour later, she passed away."[1]

My paternal great-grandparents, Gebhard and Rosalia Sagmeister

Jakob and Johanna were not particularly cursed with bad luck. This kind of misery was experienced by much of the world two hundred years ago, with only about 60 percent of children surviving into adulthood at the time.[2]

The next generation of Sagmeisters, my great-grandparents Gebhard and Rosalia Sagmeister, did not fare much better, losing five children in their lifetimes.[3] However, unlike Jakob and Johanna, they could both read and write,

DEMOCRACY I ▶

Number of democracies worldwide, 1945–2015

Antique store owned by Gebhard
and Rosalia Sagmeister

elevating them to the intellectual elite of their times. In the nineteenth century, only 15 percent of their contemporaries were literate.[4] They owned a small antique store in Bregenz, and the wares that didn't sell were stored in the attic of my childhood home. The initial historical paintings for the work shown in this book came directly from this attic and were originally for sale in Gebhard and Rosalia Sagmeister's shop.[5]

My grandmother Josefine was the first woman in my family allowed to vote. She had to wait until she was forty-two years old, as voting rights for women in Austria began in 1918.

While so much of this data can at first be read as distant sets of numbers, if we consider our own family history, we can begin to make the connections between these numbers and how life has improved for many of us, my own family included.

My paternal
grandmother,
Josefine
Sagmeister

1   Meinrad Pichler, *Sagmeister: Geschichten einer Bregenzer Familie* (self-pub., Bregenz: 1998), 28.
2   "Child Mortality," *Gapminder*, November 10, 2017, www.gapminder.org/question_tag/child-mortality.
3   Meinrad Pichler, *Sagmeister: Geschichten einer Bregenzer Familie*, 46.
4   Max Roser and Esteban Ortiz-Ospina, "Literacy," *Our World in Data*, August 13, 2016, www.ourworldindata.org/literacy.
5   Most of the subsequent pieces were bought from small auction houses in Austria, Germany, Belgium, Holland, Italy, and the United Kingdom.

◀ FAMINE I

Famine victims worldwide,
1860 vs. 2000

THE WORLD IS TERRIBLE. The world is fantastic. Both statements are true. Which one I choose to believe depends very much on the time frame through which I look at the world. If I observe it from the perspective of a single day, while I'm writing this on August 4, 2022, I read that four people were struck by lightning in a park close to the White House in Washington, DC, killing three.[1] If I step back and widen my time frame to a hundred years, a different picture emerges: in 1920, five hundred Americans were killed by lightning. By 2022, this has been steadily reduced to fewer than thirty per year.[2] Considering we're now experiencing worse storms, and the population has tripled in the past century, this is remarkable. Of course, this progress will ultimately mean very little if we're all going to become

◀ MOWING AND BLOWING

Amount of ozone-depleting pollution generated by leaf blowers vs. passenger cars, 2020

extinct in a giant heat wave. Global warming is the biggest challenge of our lifetime. A global scientific consensus exists that this warming has been created by humans and therefore will have to be solved by humans. Out of 69,406 authors of peer-reviewed scientific articles, only four now believe that global warming has not been caused by us.[3]

We are currently dumping forty billion tons of carbon dioxide (CO_2) into the atmosphere each year, an almost unimaginably high number that is difficult to wrap one's head around.[4] Expressed differently, we are discarding eighty trillion (80,000,000,000,000) pounds into the airspace surrounding our world. To imagine this as a solid form, this amount of high-density CO_2 would take the shape of twenty cubic miles.

We need to differentiate between strategies that would eliminate a single ton, 100 tons, 100,000 tons, and 100 million tons of CO_2.

Sadly, these analogies do little to clarify the problem. We know that if we continue down this path, the temperature of Earth will increase about 7.2 degrees Fahrenheit (4°C) by the end of the century, resulting in heatwaves, severe droughts, and major floods of increasing intensity.[5]

To begin counteracting the damage done, we need to decrease the yearly temperature to an absolute maximum of 3.6 degrees Fahrenheit (2°C). To achieve this, we will have to cut our CO_2 output in half by the middle of this century and eliminate it completely by the end of the century. This will be extremely difficult to achieve, as fossil fuels currently provide over 80 percent of all energy used in the world.[6] Our thirst for energy is huge, and fossil fuels are convenient and enjoy well-established infrastructure to support their creation and use. The

◀ CARBON II

Carbon footprint of protein-rich foods per roughly two pounds (1 kg) of protein, 2018

denial of the problem on the political right as well as technology phobia on the left only compound the problem.

In order to help save our planet, we must make sacrifices. However, the idea that the world population will stop traveling, renounce heating, and forgo affordable food and clothing, while simultaneously eliminating the production of cement and steel, is simply not realistic.

We need to figure out how to create the highest levels of usable energy while producing the lowest levels of greenhouse gases. We also need to differentiate between strategies that would eliminate a single ton, 100 tons, 100,000 tons, or 100 million tons of CO_2.

The atmosphere belongs to no one person; it belongs to all of us. We need to charge people and corporations for the waste they carelessly discard. Otherwise, energy-dense fossil fuels will continue to enjoy an advantage over other, more environmentally conscious techniques.

Forty years ago, I played a tiny part in the antinuclear power movement in Austria that prevented a recently constructed reactor in Zwentendorf from ever being used, eliminating the adoption of nuclear power in my home country to this day.

I changed my mind in the meantime. The new, compact nuclear power station designs are much safer and more efficient, and produce far less waste. These designs are as different from the Zwentendorf model as a Smart car is from a Ford Model T. Compared to all other energy sources, nuclear power uses the smallest footprint, creates the most energy, and is the safest.[7] During the largest nuclear

FILTHY RICH ▶

Percentage of global
emissions by income
class, 1990–2015

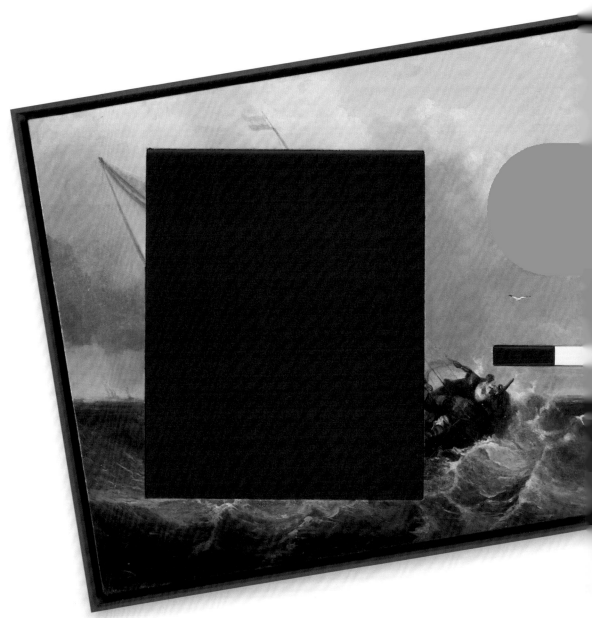

accidents in the past, thirty-one people died in Chernobyl (1986), one person died in Fukushima (2011), and thankfully no one perished at Three Mile Island (1979). However, more than one thousand people have died from cancer as a result of

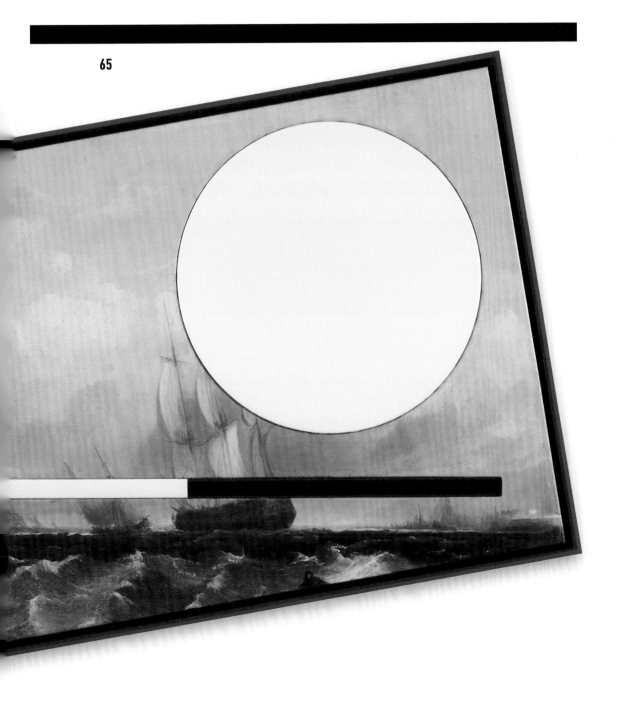

these events, and this number will likely grow as survivors age. Today, people are 243 times more likely to be killed by petroleum fuels than by nuclear power, and around one million people die every year from health complications related to the air pollution coal produces. If these numbers sound unbelievable to you, I am not surprised, because they initially felt hard for me to accept too.

The Chicago world's fair in 1893 exhibited some of the most revolutionary ideas of its time. Yet when experts were asked what the dominant technology in the twentieth century would be, a mere seven years away, nobody guessed the car or the telephone.[8]

The speed of technological invention has increased remarkably over the past 125 years. To begin healing our world, we will need enormous breakthroughs in the efficiencies of batteries and smart grids, reducing energy waste and more fully harnessing the power of renewable sources. In order to curb CO_2 emissions, we will have to develop decarbonizing methods to implement in the production of cement, fertilizer, and steel, industries responsible for nearly half of all global emissions.[9] Of the many ideas on the table, I found the genetic engineering of wheat, corn, and other food crops particularly interesting.[10] The stalk grows its roots downward instead of sideways. Instead of composting and releasing CO_2 back into the air, this kind of deep-rooted crop would keep CO_2 in the ground as trees do. Farmers will be motivated to adopt this strategy, as carbon-rich soils require less fertilizer.

Unprecedented incentives to solve global warming are now on offer. One of the most prestigious goals in the sciences is finding the cure for cancer. Arguably, the fame and fortune to be showered on scientists achieving significant advances in solving global warming would be even more magnificent, as this issue directly imperils us all.

The economist Paul Romer differentiates between *complacent optimism*, a child passively waiting for presents, and *conditional optimism*, a child wishing for a treehouse who then seeks out materials and their peers to help them build it.[11]

I am *conditionally optimistic* we will be able to overcome this.

1   McKenna Oxenden, "Lightning Hit Kills Three in Capital," *New York Times*, August 4, 2022, www.nytimes.com/2022/08/04/us/white-house-lightning.

2   Hannah Ritchie, Pablo Rosado, and Max Roser, "Natural Disasters," *Our World in Data*, December 7, 2022, www.ourworldindata.org/natural-disasters#lightning.

3   Gavin Stern, "Fifty Years After U.S. Climate Warning, Scientists Confront Communication Barriers," *Science*, November 27, 2015, www.science.org/doi/10.1126/science.350.6264.1045.

4   "Global CO_2 Emissions Tracker," *The World Counts*, www.theworldcounts.com/challenges/climate-change/global-warming/global-co2-emissions.

5   World Bank Group. "New Report Examines Risks of 4 Degree Hotter World by End of Century." *World Bank*, March 18, 2013, www.worldbank.org/en/news/press-release/2012/11/18new-report-examines-risks-of-degree-hotter-world-by-end-of-century.

6   Hannah Ritchie, "How Have the World's Energy Sources Changed over the Last Two Centuries?," *Our World in Data*, December 1, 2021, www.ourworldindata.org/global-energy-200-years.

7   Matt Ridley, *The Rational Optimist: How Prosperity Evolves* (New York: HarperCollins, 2010), 345.

8   Ridley, *The Rational Optimist*, 346.

9   Samantha Gross, "The Challenge of Decarbonizing Heavy Industry," *Brookings*, June 2021, www.brookings.edu/research/the-challenge-of-decarbonizing-heavy-industry.

10 If my advocacy of genetic engineering comes as a shock to you, please read this open letter signed by more than one hundred Nobel Prize laureates: "Laureates Letter Supporting Precision Agriculture (GMOs)," *Support Precision Agriculture*, June 29, 2016, www.supportprecisionagriculture.org/nobel-laureate-gmo-letter_rjr.html.

11 Akshat Rathi, "Why the Newest Nobel Laureate Is Optimistic about Beating Climate Change," *Quartz*, October 8, 2018, www.qz.com/1417222/why-new-nobel-laureate-paul-romer-is-optimistic-about-beating-climate-change.

CORN/RICE/WHEAT ▶

Left: Number of acres planted with grains, 1965 vs. 2005
Right: Amount of global corn, rice, and wheat harvest, 1965 vs. 2005

◀ CARBON I

Cumulative emissions of CO_2 into the atmosphere, 1751–2015

OIL ▲

Number of large oil spills worldwide, 1975–2015

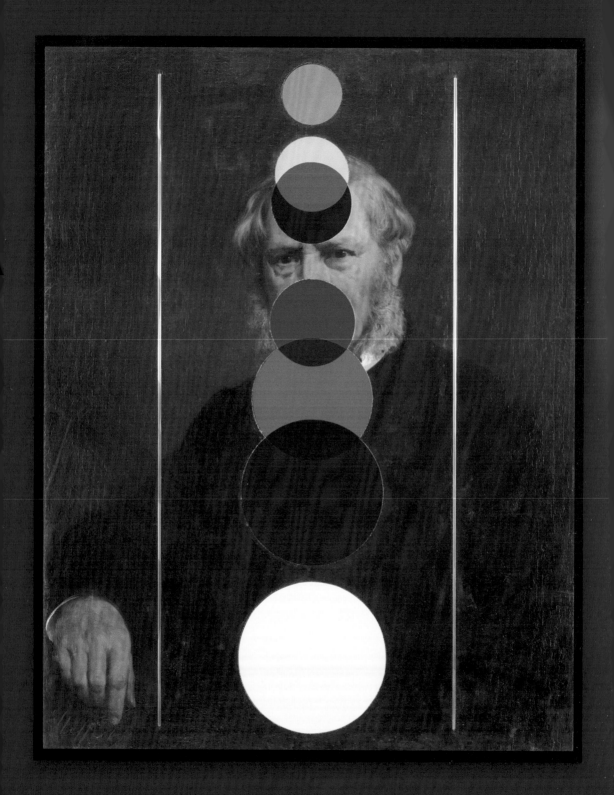

Design by the Numbers
Steven Heller

Numbers are the essential workers in our world's information systems, or what Marshall McLuhan dubbed the "Gutenberg Galaxy." Conceiving of a world without numerical systems is impossible. Just listing the following quotidian uses of numbers is breathtaking: dates, times, weather, weights, currency, geography, measurements, identification, and, of course, all types of data, data, and much more data . . . The absence of numerals would create a vacuum so vast that even hypothetically considering such a possibility triggers panic.

◀ MONEY TO LEARN

Public education spending in developed nations as a percentage of GDP, 1880–2000

But what if, for the sake of argument, numbers as we know them were replaced by a new comprehensive quantification system that would allow numerical data to be understood in a more efficient way? This is, I believe, one of Stefan Sagmeister's goals with his latest project.

Whether his approach—making comparative shapes to represent numerical statistics—will change perceptions or cause a paradigm shift in a field rife with conventions, only time will tell. But alternative data presentation techniques have been successfully introduced by visual data experimenters before (for instance Otto Neurath and Rudolf Modley), and their designs have become the norm. For now, Sagmeister's ambitious approach is an outlier that certainly questions the durability and credibility of the mass of numerical data that is unremittingly dumped into our real and virtual worlds.

Sagmeister's work forces viewers to think about the role of numbers and the ways they are designed, and by who. Arguably, the details of letters get more attention than do numbers.

In the design process, numerals seem almost to be taken for granted. Typefaces and letters are designed to give concrete form to words that make ideas accessible. Numbers are part of that equation.

The designer of type fonts must think holistically. Letters and punctuation marks are not the only characters in a fully functional typeface; numerals are equal members of any type family, not first or second cousins. Characters—from A to zero—carry the same weight. In fact, numerals are arguably the most critical component because of their universality across many languages.

Numbers are shapes, and shapes translate into words. While most languages have different words that indicate their value, to avoid global confusion most number signs are consistent (in English *one* = 1; Spanish *uno* = 1; German *eins* = 1; and Chinese *yī* = 1). This does not mean that creativity, in regard to the aesthetics or beauty of numbers, is held hostage to a universal linguistic or symbolic standard.

Numbers are symbols. There are many alphabetic systems and, like language, general

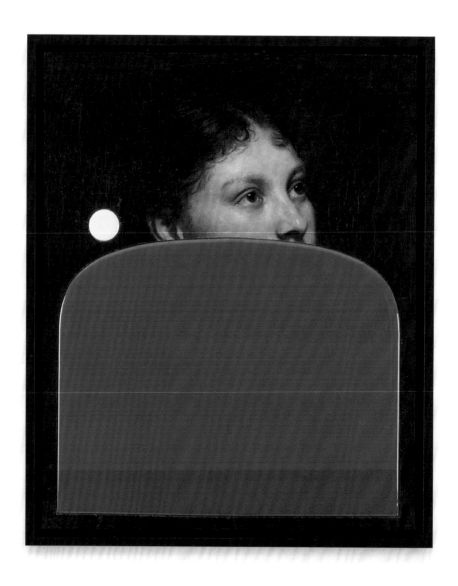

BABIES

Women in the United States
dying in childbirth per 100,000
pregnant women, 1915 vs. 2015,
visualized in a historical painting
and on a cotton shirt

fluency is based on consensus. Likewise sets, sequences, and codes of numbers are comprehensible only if the people or machines using them concur on their meaning.

A system is not a style. The design of numerals has long been the province of the typeface designer or graphic designer. Most type families are categorized by appearances, such as scripts, serifs, sans serifs, Gothics, and grotesques, that also include numbers with harmonious characteristics. Letters and numerals are created as either one-of-a-kind drawings or as multiple-use fonts; whatever the end result, if the numbers conform to the same system, they will have similar physical properties and render the same outcomes.

Sagmeister is not content with *sameness*. His modus operandi is to challenge conventions and disprove clichéd assumptions. By way of example, every seven years, like clockwork, he takes a yearlong sabbatical from whatever he has accomplished during the previous seven and uses it to recharge and discover what he will spend the next seven years learning, conceiving, and making. (Over the past two decades, he's intimately explored themes of happiness and beauty, resulting in talks, books, and exhibitions.)

Now Is Better focuses on Sagmeister's iconoclastic conceptions regarding data visualization. He combines art, design, history, and statistical analysis to create a visual language that imparts one central truth: humanity on the whole is better off politically, economically, societally, and culturally now than we were decades, centuries, and millennia before. And in the process, he wants to prove that his analytical visual methods, although abstract on the surface, have the virtue of longer and greater staying power than the tsunami of up-to-the-minute information resulting in the graphic data deluge on the screens of our relentlessly updated smart devices. As Sagmeister tells Hans Ulrich Obrist elsewhere in this volume, for the *Now Is Better* project he sought out a medium—historical oil paintings—on which he could make bold interventions using variously sized geometric shapes

IN THE KITCHEN ▶

Percentage of people in the United States who believe that women should return to their traditional roles in society, 1990–2010, visualized on a trench coat and in a historical painting

rather than actual numerals, which graphically express and proportionately symbolize quantifiably factual data through shape, color, and size.

Sagmeister's alternative approach to data visualization—which includes a piece designed to show that two hundred years ago, only one democratic country existed, while today ninety-six countries qualify as democratic—is unique in the annals of graphic design yet consistent with the contemporary requirements of design to access data in innovative ways.[1]

What distinguishes Sagmeister's work from past and present data visualization is, first of all, its tactility—everything is handmade. Second is his avoidance of literal imagery in favor of puzzle-like colors, shapes, and forms cut into antique paintings.

From the founding of visual statistics movements in the early twentieth century, sign-symbols were created to represent the subjects under examination. The leading pioneer, Otto Neurath, an Austrian sociologist who "invented" the ISOTYPE (International System of Typographic Picture Education),

HOT AND COLD ▶

Percentage of households in the United States with running water, 1900–2000

used simplified, solid pictographic silhouettes of men, women, children, cars, and ships (among others) to showcase complex data. Rather than traditional line or bar charts on a vertical/horizontal axis or overly rendered illustrations, Neurath's system provided a user-friendly shorthand for data designers and statistical visualizers that is still used today to indicate everyday needs, such as men's, women's, and all-gender bathrooms.

Sagmeister's work is more abstract than Neurath's pictograms but no less compelling, once his distinctive visual language is decoded. This work is at once art object (to hang on a wall) and information graphic (to appear on the screen or printed page), expressing emotion and serving a function. This binary quality is what makes it unique in the context of the current information-age visual frenzy—examples of which run the gamut from no-nonsense to ironic, typographic, or illustrative—and is consistent within the groove of Sagmeister's compulsively investigational body of work, through which he exhibits his predilection for making more rather than less.

◀ DIVISIONS

Left: Usage of all habitable land for agricultural purposes worldwide, 2020
Right: Percantages of land used, daily protein supply, and daily calorie supply, meat and dairy vs. plants, 2020

The front and back of a historical painting used in the *Now Is Better* series, removed from its stretcher, before inserts and restoration ▶

WE LOVE BAD NEWS. While studying communication design at Pratt Institute in Brooklyn in 1987, the front pages of the New York newspapers were all filled with the same story, about a barge carrying three thousand tons of garbage being turned away by landfills up and down the Atlantic coast. The newly labeled gar-barge dominated the headlines for weeks. The papers predicted that we were all about to disappear in one giant garbage heap in the not-so-distant future.[1]

Forty years later, we're still here. Through strategies like recycling, compacting, digitization, and the creation of new landfills, the problem of discarding our garbage has disappeared from the headlines.

In the 1970s, many thinkers believed the greatest threat to the human species was overpopulation.

◀ **CRIMINALS**

Breakdown of different crimes committed by male vs. female perpetrators in the United States, 2011

Stanford professor Paul Ehrlich warned in his bestseller *The Population Bomb* that by the 1980s, four billion people would starve to death.

Today almost no one believes in the threat of overpopulation to this extent. The United Nations predicts the world population will begin to gradually decrease by 2070. In many wealthy nations, we are already seeing naturally shrinking populations due to slowing birth rates.

Whenever a catastrophe occurs, we read about it on the front page. When that same event ceases to be troublesome, the news about its improvement is pushed toward the back of the paper, if published at all.

Long-term improvement happens in small increments and therefore does not lend itself to short-term news cycles. If the stock market improves by 0.1 percent every day over the period of a year, it will not be considered news, but if it suddenly declines by 50 percent on a single day, this will be front-page news.

News is about things that happen, not about things that don't happen. We've never heard a TV reporter announce: "I'm reporting from New York City, where no scandal broke today." Most journalists understand their job as the investigation of everything going wrong in the world.

The shorter the news cycle has become, the more prevalent the negative messages. A yearly almanac or monthly magazine can observe an event at a distance, heightening the chance of both positive and negative aspects being covered. By definition, hourly cable news concentrates on bad things happening right this very moment. It matters less if you are watching right-wing Fox News or left-wing MSNBC; ultimately the comparable form of the graphics and the

CRIMINALS ▶

A continuation of different crimes committed by male vs. female perpetrators in the United States, 2011

◀ ROSALIA

Percentage of children around
the world dying before reaching
the age of five, 1870–2020

READING AND WRITING

Number of children receiving an
education worldwide, per one
hundred children, 1820 vs. 2020

uniform nature of urgency overrides political differences. The medium really is the message.

If news outlets truly reported on the big changes in the world, both positive and negative, they could run the headline: "135,000 people escaped extreme poverty today, and every day, for the past 25 years."[2]

The amygdala—a small, almond-shaped mass in the central brain—compounds the problem, transporting negative messages much faster than positive ones in order to keep us safe. The brains of our prehistoric ancestors required a shortcut for negative news—it was extremely important to detect that lion quickly, as the alternative was death. The brain never developed a similar timesaver for positive messages. If the banana was missed, there might be another one around the corner. Today, we're all living much safer lives, and our lives would be better informed if we were more receptive to positive news.

If news outlets truly reported on the big changes in the world, both positive and negative, they could run the headline: "135,000 people escaped extreme poverty today, and every day, for the past 25 years."

I don't believe the people running our media outlets to be evil; they simply leverage our naturally heightened interest in drama and negative messaging. Most attempts to create a positive news site have failed immediately.[3]

Sentiment mining is a research method in which you review the news for frequently used words like "good," "terrible," and "horrific," tallying each use and its context. This research validates my gut feeling, confirming that the increasing negativity of the news over the past few decades is scientifically provable.[4]

Even when the news is reassuring, headlines find a way around it: the *New York Times* reported in 2009 that the world temperature had not risen in a decade under the headline: "Plateau in temperature adds difficulty to task of reaching a solution."[5]

We simply find drama more fascinating.

While working on *The Happy Film*, a documentary about my own happiness, our team went through the considerable trouble of sending the entire film crew from New York to Bregenz to interview my siblings. I purposefully did not take part in these interviews, as I wanted my brothers and sisters to have a chance to speak freely about all of the awful things I must have done growing up. When I checked the footage weeks later, they had talked only about positive events. This was incredibly boring. We wound up not using a single frame.

1 Dick Sheridan, "Trash Fright: Long Voyage of New York's Unwanted Garbage Barge," *Daily News*, August 14, 2017, www.nydailynews.com/new-york/trash-fight-long-voyage-new-york-unwanted-garbage-barge-article-1.812895.

2 Steve Pinker, *Enlightenment Now: The Case for Reason, Science, Humanism, and Progress* (New York: Viking, 2018), 88.

3 Adam Epstein, "Here's What Happened When a News Site Only Reported Good News for a Day," *Quartz*, December 5, 2014, www.qz.com/307214/heres-what-happened-when-a-news-site-only-reported-good-news-for-a-day.

4 Kalev Leetaru, "View of Culturomics 2.0: Forecasting Large-Scale Human Behavior Using Global News Media Tone in Time and Space," *First Monday*, August 9, 2011, www.firstmonday.org/article/view/3663/3040.

5 Matt Ridley, *The Rational Optimist: How Prosperity Evolves* (New York: HarperCollins, 2010), 295.

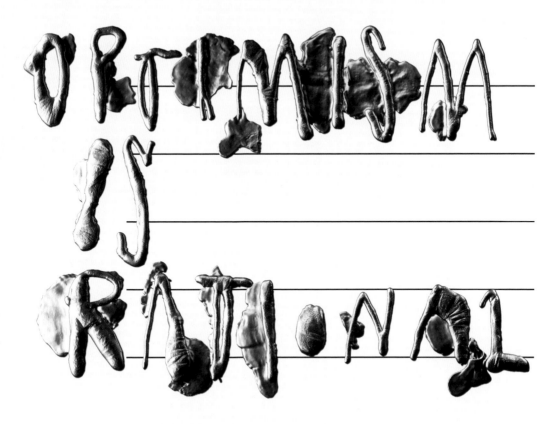

OPTIMISM IS RATIONAL. As you likely can tell by now, I am an optimist. And optimism encourages a realistic assessment of the present moment.

If the ultimate outcome of a situation can be either exceptional or terrible, and the chances of either are split evenly, then the prospects of succeeding are improved if I approach it from a bright rather than gloomy position.

And if things are better now than they were in the past—the central argument of this book—assuming things will continue to get better in the future constitutes common sense. Obviously, our world is facing issues that urgently need to be addressed, including climate change, atomic weapons, systemic inequality, and the loss of biodiversity. I believe we have a greater chance of addressing these issues if we first recognize that we've already achieved quite a lot. When I'm down or out of sorts, I'm of little use to my surroundings, to my friends, or to my family. I'm much more helpful and effective when I'm doing well.

When I examine successful campaigns resulting in behavioral change from the recent past, the tobacco-free programs in Sweden, Norway, the UK, and South Korea, all of which have significantly reduced the smoking habits of their citizens, stand out. In South Korea, the number of people who smoke has been almost cut in half, falling from 31.5 percent of the total population to 18.6 percent over the past fifteen years.[1]

In order to achieve long-term behavioral change, both the carrot and the stick have been necessary.[2] These countries implemented stick strategies, including increased taxes on tobacco, surgeon general's warnings on cigarette packaging, and bans on smoking in certain areas. On the carrot side, services supporting people who wished to stop smoking were made available, including trained professionals offering a full range of medications and aids to help control nicotine withdrawal symptoms. In South Korea, hundreds of public health centers provided smoking cessation programs and, in the long term, followed up through text and email to show support.

When it comes to reports about the state of the world, the media is doing a fantastic job providing the stick.

I'll happily provide a bit of carrot.

1   Francesca Boggio and Aleksandar Ruzicic, "The Carrot or the Stick: What Works Best for Effecting Behavioral Change to Improve Health at the Population Level?," *Executive Insight*, September 1, 2022, www.executiveinsight.ch/en/insights/publications/carrot-or-stick-what-works-best-effecting-behavioral-change-improve-health-population-level.

2   This motivational approach is made up of the "carrot" (reward for good behavior) and the "stick" (punishment for poor behavior).

MS. MP ▶

Percentage of parliamentary governments around the world which have voted in their first female representative, 1920–2020

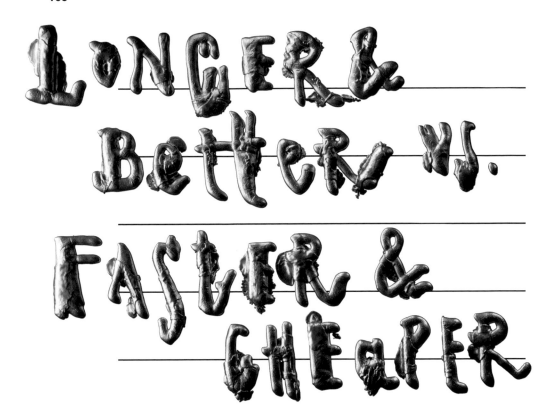

LONGER & BETTER VS. FASTER & CHEAPER. Saint Mark's Basilica in Venice is among my all-time favorite designs in the world. Its Byzantine and Renaissance interior offers such a bountiful feast for the eyes, it was only during my third visit that I made it all the way up to the main altar. After depositing an extra euro to enter, there it was: the Pala d'Oro.

This ten-by-six-and-a-half-foot wall is made of pure silver and gold, overlaid with thousands of gems and pearls. With a density of detail usually reserved for intricate jewelry, the altar was commissioned in 976 by Doge Pietro Orseolo and completed in 1345 by the goldsmith Giovanni Paolo Boninsegna, its construction taking nearly four hundred years.

The idea of starting a project today with a completion

◀ HER MONEY

Share of women in the United Kingdom in the top 10 percent of income earners, 1995–2015

"JOAN OF ARC."

date in the year 2422 seems alien to us. We want things done this year, or at least in this decade.

But there are a number of serious people exploring the benefits of long-term thinking, including Danny Hillis and Stewart Brand, cochairs of the Long Now Foundation. The mission of their nonprofit organization is to create projects and lectures that foster long-term thinking—rather than

The idea of starting a project today with a completion date in the year 2422 seems alien to us.

"faster and cheaper," they encourage us to imagine the benefits of "slower and better."

Arguably their most spectacular endeavor is the design and construction of a ten-thousand-year clock, a device that will continue to tell time ten thousand years from now. If you picture the comparatively young 4,500-year-old Egyptian pyramids and remember that they did not fulfill their primary function—to protect the graves of pharaohs—you begin to realize the complex design problems such a clock poses. The clock will be very large, built out of cheap materials (to save it from looters), and powered through a combination of sunlight and a falling weight within the clock. A working version currently ticks away at the Science Museum in London. The foundation has also built a full-sized prototype that will eventually be housed in Mount Washington near Ely, Nevada, surrounded by Great Basin National Park.[1]

Brand and Hillis want to create an apparatus so incredible that its fame will attract people from around the globe to an out-of-the-way place. This envisioned pilgrimage will encourage the contemplation of time as long-term.

With so many elements of my life seemingly gaining speed, I find reflecting upon the long term not only a soothing practice but crucial for a well-balanced existence.

◀ THIRTY-SEVEN

Hours spent at work per week in the United States, 1900 vs. 2000

1 "The Clock of the Long Now." *Long Now Foundation*, August 4, 2022. www.longnow. org/clock.

DESIGN AND ART AND POLITICS. I typically visit hundreds of exhibitions each year. The choices in Manhattan are endless—with four hundred galleries in the Chelsea neighborhood alone, and more than one thousand art spaces throughout the city, it's the ideal place to see contemporary art. In addition, I try to see as many shows as I can when traveling.

In the past decade, political art has returned with a vengeance. But numerous recent shows are seemingly preaching to the choir, concerning themselves with issues visitors would already be familiar with before they entered the gallery.[1]

Among the laudable exceptions is Nan Goldin's effective action against the sponsorship of the Sackler family at the Guggenheim and other museums—an art-world issue brought up at the right time and place. This has led to the distancing of many institutions from the family's support, including the Louvre in Paris and the Serpentine Galleries in London.[2]

The decades-old campaign by the Guerrilla Girls, an anonymous group of feminist artists, regarding the lack of equal representation in the art world has been similarly effective because the issue is now being addressed from within.

And at least one piece of political art has turned into an icon: Pablo Picasso's *Guernica* (1937) has transcended its subject of the Spanish Civil War and may be considered representative of the horrors of war in general.

The art world seems to stipulate that recent politically-minded works have to point out injustice, with positivity being positively forbidden. Carsten Höller—an artist whose work I admire—once told me that good art has to make the viewer uncomfortable. While I understand his theory, I have observed fantastic art and felt no such thing: Leonardo da Vinci's *Lady with an Ermine* (c. 1489–90) does not make me uncomfortable. Looking at an Ellsworth Kelly painting, or sitting inside a James Turrell *Skyspace*, are perfectly enjoyable experiences.[3]

Beyond our personal comfort, design has been intertwined with political history for centuries. Traditionally, design has played an enormous role in propaganda—for instance, helping visually identify both the Nazis and the Allied forces in World War II. More recently, Shepard Fairey's "Hope" poster for Barack Obama's 2008 presidential campaign, Facebook posts from Russian bots in favor of Donald Trump in a recent US election, Instagram posts in support of the LGBTQ+ community, and political buttons

WAR! ▶

Percentage of years in which the great powers have fought one another for an extended period (at least twenty-five years), 1543–2016

promoting a myriad of political positions all try to influence audiences where they live, outside of museums and galleries. Some succeed.

While the pieces represented in this book do not concern themselves with party politics, they do deal with issues of human development. Unlike much political imagery created within the world of design *or* art, these works are based not upon opinion but scientific research.[4]

As many of the pieces exemplify positive developments from our past, they might be dismissed as lightweight. Research has proven the negative critic to be perceived as more serious and intelligent than the positive critic.[5]

Oh my.

◀ **A SMALL WORLD**

Number of visitors to the
five most popular museums
in New York, 2018

1   I grew up under the adage of political art often being bad art *and* bad politics. In my experience, artists don't necessarily or automatically possess deeper insight into sociopolitical agendas.
2   Another often-quoted example would be the ACT UP campaign for AIDS awareness. To my mind, this worked so well with the tools of design—logos and posters—that I would additionally regard it as a design initiative.
3   The works of artists Christopher Wool and Richard Prince make me uncomfortable, but I don't think of their work as good art.
4   While some results of this research might require updating as new information becomes available— this is the nature of all science—it is markedly different from personal presumptions.
5   Teresa Amabile, "Brilliant but Cruel: Perceptions of Negative Evaluation," *Journal of Experimental Social Psychology* 19 (1983): 146–56.

HANG THESE THINGS. We tend to create ephemeral things in the studio. Our poster designs are up for a week or two, our websites are constantly being changed, and even our designs for music packaging—items that I had high hopes of becoming long-term possessions—ultimately went into landfills once CDs were largely replaced by digital streaming.

As the content of all the work within the *Now Is Better* series is based upon long-term data, it made sense to express it through a medium that can be reasonably expected to stick around for a long time.

All digital mediums were immediately dismissed: recently, a client asked us for files from two decades ago, and we had to locate them on Jaz discs, hunt down a used Jaz disc drive on eBay (our own had

◄ **SCRIPTURES**

Number of books published per one million people in the United Kingdom, 1600–2000

given up years ago), and hope that our twenty-year-old Illustrator files would still open on a current operating system.

On the other hand, antique oil paintings have proven their longevity, having successfully survived two to three centuries, so the assumption that they'll be around for another few hundred years is reasonable. Furthermore, over the past few decades, this period of art and artistic style has fallen out fashion, resulting in good availability and affordable prices. At the same time, the paintings did not need to be cheap, as most inexpensive things are thrown out quickly.

In the design world, ambiguity is often regarded critically. Some flexibility will be allowed when designing album covers—interpreting the meaning of that iconic prism on Pink Floyd's *The Dark Side of the Moon* (1973) can be intriguing—but in antiwar posters, the substance and direction of the content better be crystal clear.

I would not mind if a viewer developed their own interpretation of the data-driven forms inserted into the historical canvases.

The meaning of the pieces within this book is clearly defined. All forms are based upon historical data expressed in percentages, including annotated research sources. This kind of singularity would be considered an absolute faux pas in the art world, where multiple layers of understanding and various levels of interpretation are highly prized.

At the same time, I would not mind if a viewer developed their own interpretation of the data-driven forms inserted into the historical canvases. If someone understands a particular piece as a growth chart of their youngest daughter, or a curve predicting the status of their business, I'd actually be very pleased to discover such personal modes of understanding.

My goal for all these pieces is to ultimately be *beautiful*. The forms, shapes, colors, and textures should work in unison and be kind to the eye. Beautiful things tend to be around for longer than nonaesthetic objects, as their chances to be cared for, repaired, and restored are much higher.

The forms, shapes, colors, and textures should work in unison and be kind to the eye.

Beauty was all the rage in the nineteenth century, during which time it was frequently equated with a moral stance—if something was considered to be *beautiful*, it was also considered to be *good*. This heightened focus on beauty often led to excessive and melodramatic sentimentality.

I appreciate the decorative arts. After all, the first museum show of this body of work took place at the Museo Franz Mayer in Mexico City—a museum of design and decorative arts. Many of my artist friends find the idea of their work being used as decoration abhorrent, though I'd love it if a patron matched one of these pieces to the curtains in their living room.

To contrast the complex forms of the historical paintings, I wanted to visualize the inserted data in a simple way, using forms influenced by my artistic heroes Ellsworth Kelly and Donald Judd as well as my friend and design idol Tony Brook.

Judd desired to create artworks that just *were*, without any function. From a conceptual point of view, my goals could not be more different; I would love for these works to serve as reminders that we have already achieved something and that the general trajectory of world history is not as dreadful as the media would have us believe.[1]

The overall process of working on a series such as this is similar to how a song

Famine I, displayed in the living room of its collector ▶

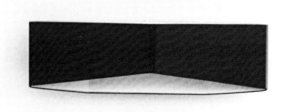

is written. When my team and I visited the bands we worked with in their rehearsal spaces, it became clear that their songs began with a combination of tiny sparks from many directions: a segment of a lyric, a guitar riff, a bass line, a particular beat.[2] Similarly, the pieces in the *Now Is Better* series could begin with the discovery of an intriguing data set, or a pleasing shape, color scheme, or composition, before combining all of these factors atop a historical painting.

Working on this series has been incredibly enjoyable. I got to explore the historical painting catalogs of smaller auction houses in Austria, Germany, Belgium, Italy, Spain, and the UK. I preselected paintings according to content, style, technique, composition, and materiality. After a satisfactory review of the condition report, I would place my bid.

On the data side, the first step was to digitally sketch out the composition, during which time dozens of directions were investigated. Using a file created from the final digital sketch, a precise MDF panel was cut on a CNC machine.[3]

Once the painting arrived in New York, it was unpacked, separated from its antique frame, measured, and photographed. It was then transported to a studio in the Brooklyn Navy Yard, where the condition of the canvas was examined before being removed from its stretcher. The un-stretched painting was then placed on a worktable and covered with tracing paper to design the shape and placement of the colorful data inserts. These shapes were then cut out of the canvas, leaving a border behind to wrap around a supporting panel. With a precut MDF panel placed underneath the canvas, heat from a hair dryer is applied to the corners

◀ *Literacy I*, displayed in the living room of its collector

Suicide I, displayed in the living room of its collector

of the painting to become malleable and bend downward around the panel. Both the canvas and MDF panel were then brushed liberally with glue and pressed together. The paintings were then brought to another Navy Yard building where the inserts were measured and cut. They were then sprayed with a clear coat of varnish and finished with epoxy resin before being fitted tightly and affixed to the MDF panel. After carefully examining the entire piece, possible cracks and chipped paint were retouched before acid-free paper was glued to the back.

This process *destroys* a historical painting. Is it disrespectful to ruin the work of another person? I answered this critical question for myself by imagining my own work being sold in the year 2222—two hundred years from now—at a small auction house in Europe. I myself would welcome the possibility of a future designer utilizing my (by then ancient) work as part of a fresh, contemporary piece for a new audience.

◀ Historical paintings in our Brooklyn studio, awaiting inserts

1 I am in contact with the people who bought
   these paintings at Thomas Erben Gallery in
   New York. Here is a quote from Hans-Joerg
   Bergler, Frankfurt, Germany: "Guests will
   generally comment on the art in my house with
   'This is nice' or 'I wouldn't want this in my
   home.' This piece is different, because people
   will ask, 'What does it mean?' and off goes an
   interesting conversation—which, in my opinion,
   is exactly what art should be about."

2 Sagmeister Inc. used to design album covers for
   bands like the Talking Heads, the Rolling Stones,
   Lou Reed, Brian Eno, and many others.

3 MDF panel: Medium-Density Fiberboard.
   CNC machine: Computer Numerical Control.
   This type of machine contains pre-programmed
   software which controls the movement of
   production equipment.

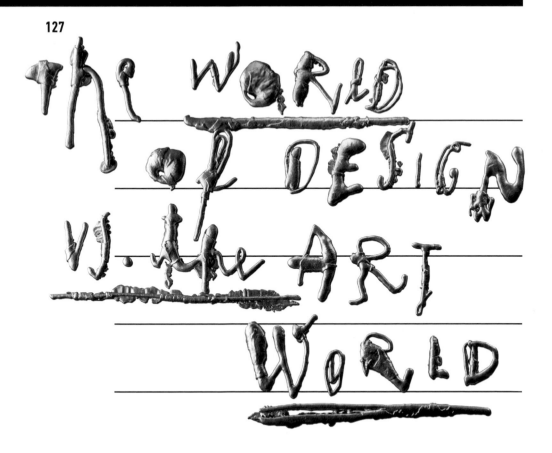

THE WORLD OF DESIGN VS. THE ART WORLD. Twenty years ago, when discussing the package design of a future album, I asked Mick Jagger about his three favorite Rolling Stones covers. He replied without any hesitation: *Exile on Main St.* (1972), *Some Girls* (1978), and *Sticky Fingers* (1971).[1] I told him we should have an easy time collaborating, as I'd have cited the exact same three covers, just in a different order: *Sticky Fingers*, *Some Girls*, then *Exile on Main St.* Stones drummer Charlie Watts leaned over to Jagger to ask: "What's on *Sticky Fingers*?" To which Jagger replied: "Oh it's the one that Andy did, the one with the zipper."

The album packaging for *Sticky Fingers* was designed by artist Andy Warhol, *Some Girls* by designer Peter Corriston, and *Exile on Main St.* by photographer Robert Frank. These three pieces of graphic design

◀ TWO MARKETS

Global art market sales vs. global sales of diapers, 2020, visualized on a t-shirt

Rolling Stones album covers, left to right: *Sticky Fingers*, 1971; *Some Girls,* 1978; and *Exile on Main St.*, 1972

were created by people in three different professions: the first by an artist, the second by a designer, and the third by a photographer who worked in between those worlds.

There's been much talk about the blurring of boundaries between art and design. I am asked in many interviews, "Do you see yourself as an artist? Or as a designer?" I can cut and paste the answers:

I went to design school. I work in a design studio. I use the language of design.

I feel comfortable in design.

I'm a designer.

However, personally I'm constantly moving back and forth between artistic and commercial spaces. I might pick up a carton of milk at the supermarket (commercial space), meet a friend for lunch (social space), and check out the new exhibition at MoMA in New York (a cultural space). Or I might buy a book with a friend at the museum store, where these three usually independent worlds merge naturally.

So why should I separate them in my professional world?

Because the world sees a world of difference.

An art studio is different from a design studio. Art is made possible through galleries, and design functions through clients. Art magazines almost never feature designers, and design blogs almost never feature artists. If I ask my artist friends about designers, they might be able to name Philippe Starck, Jony Ive, and Milton Glaser.[2] And this goes both ways—designers will know Picasso and Warhol, Jeff Koons and Damien Hirst, but only an additional few beyond that.

My favorite definition of the difference between design and art comes from one of my favorite artists, Donald Judd: "Design has to work. Art does not."[3]

In his practice, Judd separated the two disciplines according to function. All design, in order to qualify as design, has to function. If it does not function, it is not design. When I design a chair, one of my goals will need to be that it allows someone to sit down comfortably. If I push the design to the point where I can't sit on it anymore, the chair ceases to be a chair and becomes a sculpture.

Art, on the other hand, can just *be*. It does not need to do anything. At the Guggenheim in Bilbao, near one of Richard Serra's giant undulating sculptures, the museum placed a screen showing an interview with the artist. While discussing the production details of how these steel works were bent into submission in German shipyards, the interviewer asked, apropos of nothing:

"Tell me, Richard, what is the purpose of art? What is it good for?"

What a crazy, difficult question! How does one answer that?

Serra stated matter-of-factly: "The purpose of art is to have no purpose." He went on to explain that good artists create distinct worlds, and we are allowed to look into these worlds, compare them to our own, and come away with an enriched perspective. But as far as function is concerned, there is none.[4]

Théophile Gautier believed that function drags everything down into the gutter and true beauty can only be achieved if there is no function at all. When he asked himself, "What is the most functional room in the house?" he came to the conclusion that it's the bathroom—surely not the most beautiful room.[5]

So is the final conclusion that design has to function and art does not? Sadly, it's not that easy. Good design has to do more than just function. And most art does much more than just *be*.

Art = Function

When visiting contemporary galleries, I witness numerous functions of art:

Art can be used as a conversation starter or, on a purely visual level, as a backdrop for selfies.

Art can be an investment, and its function can unfortunately include money laundering. It might be utilized as a status enhancer, a vehicle for personal self-aggrandizement, or some other differentiator.

During the Renaissance, art worked hard for its reason to be, as function used to be at its very heart. It was used as decoration, economic currency, and religious or political

Left to right: Sandro Botticelli, *The Birth of Venus*, 1485–86; Leonardo da Vinci, *Portrait of a Man in Red*, 1512; Daniele da Volterra, *Michelangelo Buonarroti*, c. 1545

propaganda. Sandro Botticelli had to fit his painting *The Birth of Venus* (1485–86) into a predetermined niche in the Villa of Castello for the Medici family and prominently feature the orange tree—the patron's familial symbol and logo—in the work.[6]

In the seventeenth century, Gian Lorenzo Bernini led a giant studio employing dozens of sculptors. When he was asked to design the plaza in front of Saint Peter's Basilica in Rome, his scheme included a colonnade filled with dozens of sculptures. In many ways, the structure of his studio was more closely related to a contemporary design agency than to the romantic image of a single artist toiling away without purpose.

When considering the Italian masters of the Renaissance, Michelangelo—when not busy painting ceilings to increase Pope Julius II's fame and glory—took time out to design candlestick holders.

And when Leonardo da Vinci looked for a job, he wrote to the Duke of Milan praising his own abilities and offering, among others, the following services:

1. I have plans for strong bridges.
2. I can make an infinite number of scaling ladders.
3. I have methods for destroying fortresses.
4. I have many types of portable cannons.
5. I will assemble efficient catapults.
6. I have examples of fire-resistant ships.
7. I can conduct water from one place to another.
8. Also, I can paint.[7]

The single most famous painter in history thought his engineering skills were of more value to the duke than his artistic talents.

Design = Function

Is function all that is required of design? I'd argue that if it does not go beyond function, it is bad design. The Pruitt-Igoe housing projects in St. Louis, Missouri, were knocked down a mere twenty years after they were built, as their lack of beauty was thought to encourage vandalism and poor maintenance, which eventually made the residences unfit for habitation.[8]

They did not *function*.

The contemporary digital equivalent of the public housing project might be Twitter, the most strictly functional of all popular social media platforms, in which aesthetics play a small role. Its lack of beauty paves the way for misinformation and prejudice, discouraging many potential users from using it. It does not function as well as it could.

On the other hand, Instagram, a platform in which aesthetics plays a bigger role, is a rapidly expanding medium with three times as many active monthly users.[9]

Good Design = Function + Delight

Good design has to *help* someone. Good design has to *delight* someone.

As designers, we must try to elevate beauty to the same level as function. We can't just be problem solvers. Many of our problems are so easy to solve that pure problem solving becomes simply lazy. We need to solve design issues with delight. We must be able to create joy.

Art = Design

I'd assert that graphic design was invented in the nineteenth century by the Impressionist artist Henri de Toulouse-Lautrec. Arguably the first person to merge function and delight in a single piece of work, Toulouse-Lautrec pursued the goal of informing people while simultaneously delivering an art experience. He wrangled the job of poster design away from the printers, who had been responsible for the discipline throughout the eighteenth and nineteenth centuries. While he worked most of his life as an artist, leaving behind more than seven hundred canvases and five thousand drawings, his graphic design work for the Moulin Rouge, featuring famous performers of the age, such as dancer La Goulue or singer Yvette Guilbert, is now as iconic as any of his paintings.

Left: Gustav Klimt, poster for the First Secession Exhibition, 1898
Right: Egon Schiele, *Shaw or the Irony*, poster for a lecture by Egon Friedell, 1910

I spent my formative years in Vienna, a city in which art and design have always been close to each other and where practitioners of both insist there is no difference between the two. Famous Viennese artists of the twentieth century Gustav Klimt, Egon Schiele, and Oskar Kokoschka all painted canvases and designed posters.

In Germany, the faculty of the Bauhaus encouraged their students to be involved in the disciplines of art, architecture, and design simultaneously. Josef Albers designed furniture, tableware, and record covers in addition to being a well-known painter. Since then, only a few people have managed to successfully work in all of these fields at once.

Alexander Liberman revolutionized the modern magazine layout and also created sculptures that are now in the collections of the Guggenheim and the Metropolitan Museum of Art in New York.[10] Paula Scher is one of the most prolific corporate identity designers and also enjoys a successful career showing her map paintings in galleries.

Alternatively, artist Rachel Whiteread has created a body of work that solidifies the negative space within and under

Barbara Kruger, *I shop therefore I am*, 1987

objects. In 1991, she produced the underside of her bed in concrete, making the invisible visible. She describes this as a container of memories. Later, she produced the underside of a different bed, one she remembers from her parents' home, this time using upholstered fabric that helped make this piece of art a fully functioning piece of design. She managed to create a work that is truly both art and design.

Art > Design

Many important artists started out as designers. Barbara Kruger's philosophy-driven typographic statements were surely inspired by her multiyear career as the design director for *Mademoiselle* magazine.

And the most famous artist-designer is of course Andy Warhol. He enjoyed a successful career as a commercial illustrator, winning gold medals at the Art Directors Club of New York, before dedicating his attention to art.

Design < Art

With Warhol, the art-versus-design question becomes more complex, as he also created art in order to finance his design, painting endless portraits of titans of industry and entertainment to support his magazine, *Interview*.

Long after he established himself as an artist, he created graphic designs that are arguably of higher quality than some of the art he created to make money. And it gets even more complex: as a Pop artist, Warhol worked in opposition to his contemporaries like Willem de Kooning, Jackson Pollock, and Franz Kline, a group of macho Abstract Expressionist painters dedicated to grand, formal gestures. In a 1964 exhibition, Warhol showed half a dozen different box designs: Kellogg's corn flakes, Del Monte peach halves, Heinz tomato ketchup, Campbell's tomato juice, and the Brillo box, though only the Brillo box would become a fixture in art history textbooks and a symbol of Pop art. This might be connected to the fact that the original Brillo box was designed by the Abstract Expressionist painter James Harvey, made to help cushion his artist salary. This example can be described as a designer who became an artist (Warhol) by taking a design created by an artist who moonlighted as a designer (Harvey) and transforming it into art.

It's complicated.

Function and Function

Function does not exist as a binary proposition—it tends to vary, offering different degrees of functionality.

In architecture, a factory requires a high degree of functionality. It depends upon a variety of processes for products to be manufactured. In a religious space, such as a cathedral, there is no need for a toilet. It is a place for contemplation. Its functionalities are low.

In transportation design, a cement truck features a higher degree of functionality than a sports car. In graphic design, an income tax form requires high functionality, while the layout of a music magazine article does not.

We tend to celebrate low functionality and revere its designers. Very few readers will be familiar with the designer of the US income tax form—a culturally relevant document—while some will recognize David Carson as the designer who once typeset a double-page spread for *Ray Gun* magazine in dingbats.

Product designer Hella Jongerius once asked: "Who'd want to ruin a perfectly good vase by putting flowers in it?" While her vases are capable of functioning as traditional vases, they're not really meant to be used as such. And while her stance could be interpreted as self-involved, the concept of design without function has historical precedent.

For instance, the painted porcelain tableware set of the Bavarian court in Munich was commissioned not to be used at the dining table but to be displayed in cabinets. Similarly, many beautiful pieces of Chinese porcelain were made for display purposes only and commissioned by wealthy ruling dynasties.

In 2008, while riding a scooter in Bali during my second sabbatical, I looked for particularly beautiful roads with little traffic, allowing me to ride without a helmet, the wind rushing through my hair and my favorite music playing in my ears.

During these rides, I experienced moments of pure happiness. The final important ingredient in this mix of scooter, road, wind, music, and landscape was the idea of *no purpose*.

Whenever I have to go somewhere—when the trip has purpose—moments of sheer happiness are few. *Uselessness* is necessary in the creation of *joy*.[11]

A pleasurable scooter ride represents the opposite of a commute, offering zero utility but scoring high in delight. A commute, on the other hand, contains high functionality but low levels of joy.

Given this, we appreciate spaces and processes with little usefulness. Religion once played a big role in a low-utility world, serving as part of our lives that can just be and does not have to achieve much of anything. Meditation touches this space as well, and contemporary art is also firmly situated there.

Low Functionality

In my own design practice, I've always been drawn to objects, images, and spaces with low functionality.

This is why I was attracted to designing album covers. While a cover protects the vinyl record or CD from scratches, that functionality might also be achieved by any old piece of cardboard. While album designs function as perceptible signifiers for the music and aid promotion, they leave plenty of room for individual expression and visualized emotion.

Very Low Functionality

The series of typographic projects titled *Things I have learned in my life so far* contains very little function. It was financed

Trying to look good limits my life, 2004

by clients who allowed my studio to insert insights from my diary into their media.

Trying to look good limits my life. We created these billboards for a French arts organization just outside of Paris, in which I visually wonder if my desire to always come across as a nice guy fences me in.

Having guts always works out for me was created for the Austrian magazine *.copy*. It's the one maxim that I do have difficulty adhering to: even though I often overcome my fears, I still have to talk myself into it every time. I do tend to do get better at approaching whatever the obstacle may be once I've overcome it a couple of times in a row. But then I fall out of it again.

Keeping a diary supports personal development was commissioned by the Singapore Film Office. It was displayed on film production websites and on a giant LED screen in a busy commercial setting. It performed a promotional function and

Having guts always works out for me, 2003

the client received press from it, but no logo or advertising message was included.

All of these pieces are *design*. Significant difficulties had to be overcome in order to get them shown in magazines and in public advertising. Displaying them on gallery walls would have been much easier.[12] And of course, ultimately function and non-function will always be rendered in many shades of gray, never in pure black or white. Philosopher Theodor Adorno once said: "Freedom from purpose and purposeful-ness can never be absolutely separated from each other. There is no chemically pure purposefulness. Even the most pure forms of purpose are nourished by ideas, like formal trans-parency, which in fact are derived from artistic experience."[13] Ultimately it is impossible to create pure functionality—or, conversely, something that contains no function whatsoever.

Keeping a diary supports personal development, 2006

Good Artists Creating Bad Designs

I love the work of Donald Judd. Several of his prints adorn my living room, and his recent show at MoMA in New York was one of the most exhilarating exhibitions I've seen in the past few years. And yet, I have five nieces, six nephews, seven grandnieces, and eight grandnephews, and I can't imagine any of them of them happily sleeping in his minimalistic design for a children's bed.

Good Designers Creating Bad Art

Designers of a certain age sometimes feel they can't be bothered with client problems and the accompanying annoyances anymore. They begin to create art. Unfortunately, many good designers transform into bad artists. Lucian Bernhard, one of the originators of the modern poster style in the 1920s and

1930s, created rather awful sculptures later in life. They still show up at auction, such as his nude Ariadne figure that sold for $240. The value of its bronze-colored composite material alone might be higher.

In the 1930s, designer Lester Beall established a modern, primary-color-based style that was completely his own. His posters were unique. His later drawings and paintings borrowed heavily from Pollock and de Kooning. And one of the absolute giants of American graphic design, Paul Rand, painted sad canvases derivative of artist Paul Klee's works.

I have taken part in portfolio reviews at elite design schools and encountered a number of students who have avoided the difficulty of creating a good piece of design by making bad art. I have witnessed several iterations of shaky videos of sidewalks, seemingly shot on the way from the dorms to class. No art gallery would show this work, and no design company would offer to hire this person.

Democracy, Fairness, and Justice

By the 1980s, performance artist Scott Burton was fed up with the art world. He felt it had become a cult, purely concerned with creating a language legible for a select few and making art inaccessible for most people as a result.[14] He wanted to bring social meaning and public relevance back into art and began designing what he referred to as *pragmatic structures*, chair-like sculptures you could sit on. His work was distinguishable from that of designers, as his chairs did not have to follow the laws of common sense or practicality.

Compared to the output of the art world, design tends to be more democratic. As most designed objects can be endlessly reproduced, they are more affordable and within the comprehension of a wider and more diverse audience.

——

By the 1980s, performance artist Scott Burton was fed up with the art world. He felt it had become a cult, purely concerned with creating a language legible for a select few and making art inaccessible for most people as a result.

——

The initial print run of Jay-Z's album *Kingdom Come* (2006), for which we designed the cover, reached five million copies. Not even the most widely distributed publication in the art world can connect to such a large and non-elitist audience.

In the world of design, we tend to deal with clients who are by and large professionals. Sagmeister Inc. has created hundreds of designs over the past thirty years. In general, our clients did what they promised to do, and we got paid.[15]

In contrast, my artist friends talk about gallery owners who start out because they love art. After a couple of years they discover it to be a real business, and over time some succumb to money pressures: they become crookish. My friends also share horror stories about prints being mysteriously sold with no money transferred, or discovering a painting at a collector's house without having been notified of its sale.

In the art world, cheating can be legal, as displayed in the tactic of chandelier bidding employed by many auction houses. Chandelier bidding is an innocent term for the auctioneer looking out over the audience and declaring a supposed bid— $1.4 million, $1.5 million, $1.6 million—when no one had been raising their hand. The person who winds up paying $1.6 million overpays by at least $100,000. In every other world, this is would be called *fraud*.[16]

TWO MARKETS ▸

Global art market sales vs. global sales of diapers, 2020

A Phone vs. a Sculpture

Because of wider distribution, design objects tend to have a bigger impact.

Compare one of the most influential design products from the past few decades, the iPhone, with one of the most influential pieces of art from the same period, Jeff Koons's *Balloon Dog* (1993), or Damien Hirst's shark preserved in formaldehyde.[17] While more than two billion iPhones have been sold, only three *Balloon Dog* works have been purchased.[18] From whatever angle you look at it, the influence of Koons's work on our lives pales in comparison.

Let's try to consider the quality of these pieces. Judging the iPhone would include subjective elements such as shape, form, color, and materiality as well as more objective features such as the phone's sound and camera quality, or the accessibility of its interface. The camera either delivers sharp images or not, the interface is either intuitive or not.

Determining the subjective qualities of *Balloon Dog*—as it does not need to serve any objective function—proves to be more elusive. In the art world, the number of gatekeepers who determine what is good and what is not tends to be small. A prominent New York gallerist I know think it's as low as two hundred people worldwide.

If two hundred museum directors, gallerists, curators, critics, collectors, academics, and artists are empowered to be in charge of this global narrative, the possibilities for shenanigans and market maniupulations are plentiful. Insider trading becomes irresistible. And in art it *is* legal.

If the rules of the financial industry applied to the art world, all of its players would be in prison: artists, gallerists, and collectors. In contrast, a much larger group of people around the world influence who gets to be on top in the design world. Hundreds of thousands of users, based upon their attention spans and purchase habits, determine who belongs in the top tier of the profession.

If I look at the ruling stars in the design and architecture world, while I appreciate the work of some much more than others, I have to admit they are all talented and work hard.

> **If the rules of the financial industry applied to the art world, all of its players would be in prison: artists, gallerists, and collectors.**

If I were to review a list of the biggest names in the art world, I'd be surprised by seeing a number of those artists so highly ranked. I once asked the chief curator of a major New York museum why she was setting up a retrospective with one of these top artists, and she told me it was because he is important. When I asked why he is important, she could not respond with a satisfactory answer.

The Issue with Branding

I have long believed in the impact of branding in the design world and thought its power in art to be minimal. For example, if I compare a packaged consumer product like aspirin, the branded version from Bayer costs $17.90, while the generic version goes for $4.50. The consumer is willing to pay four times as much for the trust and security they feel they get when buying from an established company.

BEING SOCIAL ▸

Percentage of GDP spent on social programs in the United States, 1920–2020

In the realm of high-end fashion accessories, one can spend more than eight thousand dollars for an original Birkin bag from Hermès—if you can get your hands on one—or buy a similar looking knockoff for under two hundred dollars. For the privilege of owning the branded version from Hermès, you are spending forty times as much, possibly the highest multiple you'll encounter in the world of product design.

By comparison, one can spend $91.1 million for a balloon animal sculpture from Jeff Koons, even though a Chinese knock-off is available for about two thousand dollars.[19] In this case you choose to spend forty thousand times as much in order to get the original, branded version. The buyer pays for the brand of the artist who made it, Jeff Koons; the brand of his gallery, Gagosian; the brand of the collector who owned it, David Rockefeller; the brand of the museum who exhibited it, MoMA; and the brand of the auction house who sold it, Christie's.

Even though the world of design is perceived to be more commercial than the art world, when it comes to money matters, design ultimately proves to be more straightforward, egalitarian, and diverse.

1 On *Sticky Fingers*, the actual zipper attached to the front cover not only scratched all the other albums in its vicinity, but also raised the question of whether you'd see Mick Jagger naked on the inner sleeve. (You did not.)

2 Philippe Starck is arguably the most prominent designer of the past few decades. He created products, interiors, and architecture, and is credited with the invention of the boutique hotel. Jony Ive was the chief design officer at Apple for almost two decades, creating such classics as the iMac, the iPod, and the iPhone. Milton Glaser was an American graphic designer and a cofounder of *New York Magazine* and Push Pin Studios. He also created the I♥NY symbol.

3 Donald Judd, quoted in Barbara Bloemink, *Design Is Not Art: Functional Objects from Donald Judd to Rachel Whiteread* (London: Merrell, 2004).

4 Richard Serra, interview by Charlie Rose. *Charlie Rose*. December 27, 2013, www.youtube.com/watch?v=gNI6VxaExsQ.

5 Théophile Gautier, Preface of *Mademoiselle de Maupin* (Philadelphia, 1835; Project Gutenberg, May 8, 2015), www.gutenberg.org/files/48893/48893-0.txt.

6 Medici's Villa of Castello was owned by a branch of the Medici family from the mid-fifteenth century to the late eighteenth century. The orange tree is said to have had this association on account of the assonance between the family name and the name of the orange tree, which at the time was *mala medica*.

7 "Leonardo Da Vinci's Handwritten Resume, 1482," *Open Culture*, January 22, 2014, www.openculture.com/2014/01/leonardo-da-vincis-handwritten-resume-1482.html.

8 "The Life And Design Of Pruitt-Igoe," *MIT School of Architecture*, www.sap.mit.edu/article/standard/vertical-city-life-and-design-pruitt-igoe.

9 Sriparna Das, "Twitter vs Instagram: Which Platform You Should Be On?," *LinkedIn*, August 14, 2021, www.linkedin.com/pulse/twitter-vs-instagram-which-platform-you-should-sriparna-das; "Biggest Social Media Platforms 2022," *Statista*, July 26, 2022, www.statista.com/statistics/272014/global-social-networks-ranked-by-number-of-users.

10 Liberman worked at *Vogue* from 1962 to 1994.

11 Many years ago, we created an installation for the Chicago Cultural Center celebrating this uselessness: *Uselessness Is Gorgeous*.

12 After collaborating as partners for eight years, in 2019 Jessica Walsh and I decided to move all the commercial work over to her side of the firm. While I believe it to be paramount that people who care about design are involved in functional or commercial design—as this kind of design influences the look and feel of our world—I felt I had done my share in this space and could move on.

13 Theodor Adorno, "Functionalism Today," lecture, Deutscher Werkbund, Berlin, October 3, 1965.

14 Bloemink, *Design Is Not Art*, 53–58.

15 With the exception of Aerosmith.

16 Robin Pogrebin and Kevin Flynn, "As Art Values Rise, So Do Concerns about Market's Oversight," *New York Times*, January 27, 2013, www.nytimes.com/2013/01/28/arts/design/as-art-market-rise-so-do-questions-of-oversight.html.

17 Damien Hirst, *The Physical Impossibility of Death in the Mind of Someone Living* (1991).

18 And likely a couple of thousand knockoffs and reproductions.

19 In 2019, Christie's sold Koons's sculpture *Rabbit* (1986) for $91.1 million with fees, breaking the record at auction for a work by a living artist.

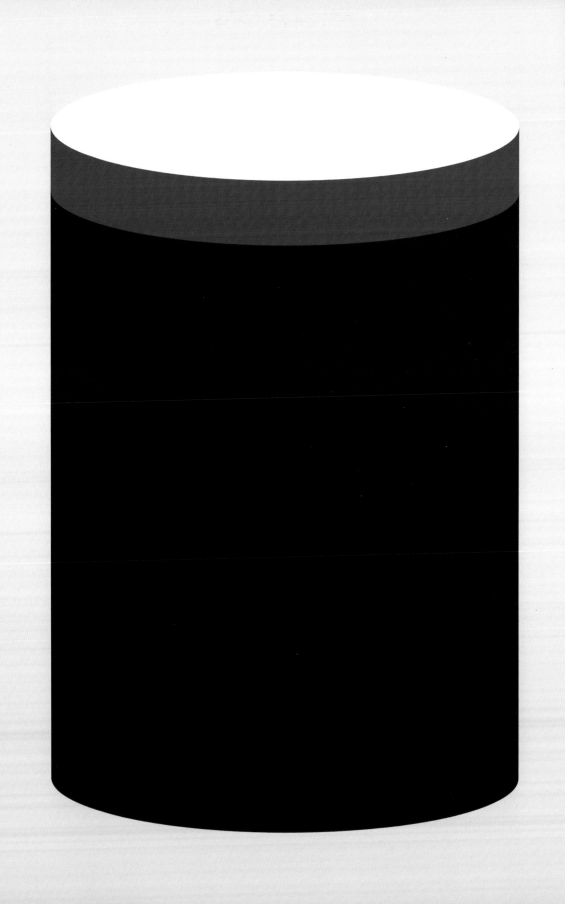

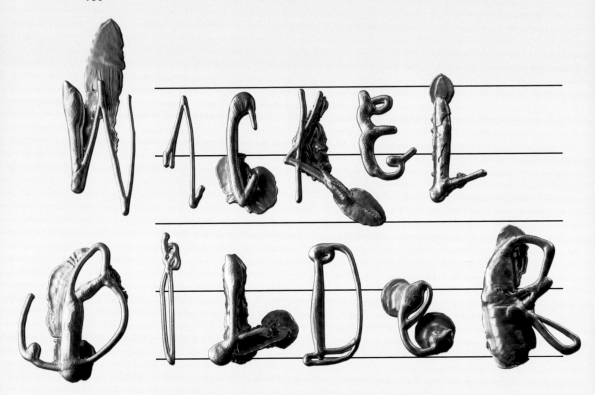

WACKELBILDER. I titled my master's thesis "Amazing, Exciting, Spectacular: Gimmicks in Design," having studied many such schemes during my time at the Pratt Institute in New York. This four-hundred-page tome includes extraordinary examples of analog inventions that can be inexpensively manufactured in large quantities—from 3D glasses and pop-up books to scratch-and-sniff stickers and a magic powder containing sea monkeys.[1] I interviewed dozens of designers who had employed such devices in the past, including Tibor Kalman and Seymour Chwast.[2]

Lenticular images, one such spectacular illusion, have been particularly close to my heart ever since. By the time these images were produced on a commercial scale in the 1960s, the technique was generally utilized for cheap postcards depicting Jesus opening

◀ **INEQUALITY**

Opposite: Income inequality in the United States, 1900
Page 155: Income inequality in the United States, 1966

and closing his eyes or Mary appearing in a shrine of curiously dimensional depth. While the appearance felt tacky, the technology was very clever. The outermost layer of the image— a ribbed plastic laminate with a series of extremely long, thin lenses—is designed to denote the illusion of movement or depth. In a two-frame animation (the opening and closing of eyes, for example), one image with eyes closed (A) and one image with eyes open (B) are sliced into thin strips. The first thin strip of image A is then placed alongside the first thin strip of image B, and so on in an alternating pattern. Atop this image collage, the thin lenses of the outermost layer, measuring the same width as the strips, reveals image A or image B, depending on the extreme angle at which you view the print.

By the 1960s, the lenticular technique was generally utilized for cheap postcards depicting Jesus opening and closing his eyes or Mary appearing in a shrine of curiously dimensional depth.

Ingenious.

Over the years, lenticular technology has improved through higher-quality lenses and tighter spacing between the image strips and lenses, with some manufacturers offering the inclusion of twenty-four "frames," allowing for smooth animation.

I've long wanted to use the technique outside of a mass-market context. I also wanted to get away from the high-density imagery usually employed in this medium to avoid ghosting.[3] Parallax Printing in Michigan—a company run by artists with a fantastic talent for exact color reproduction—is able to manufacture large-format lenticular prints and faithfully rendered one of my minimal designs through brilliant tones while significantly reducing the appearance of ghosting.

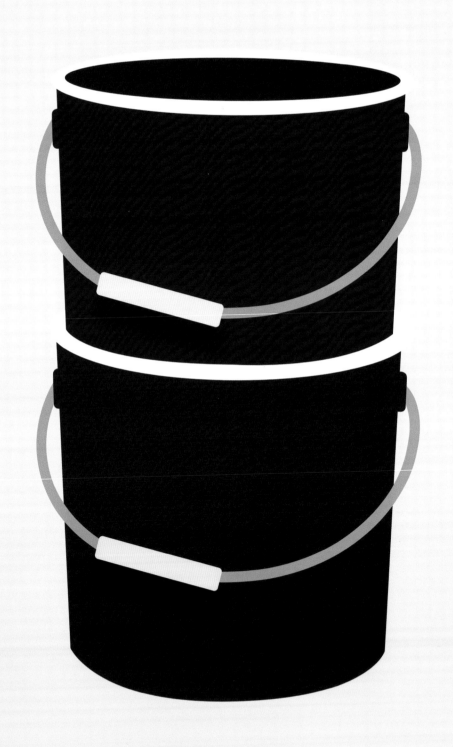

The lenticulars were created in editions of six and measured forty-six by sixty inches We also created a smaller version in editions of one hundred. While we would have loved to work with Parallax to produce the lenticular inserted into the front flap of this book, the cost sadly proved to be prohibitive.[4]

Hours spent at work per week in Europe and the United States combined, 1900

WORKING AT HOME ▶

Left: Hours spent on household work per week worldwide, 2020
Right: Hours spent on household work per week worldwide, 1900

Pages 160-61: Installation view of three lenticular prints, Thomas Erben Gallery, New York, 2021 ▶▶

1   The powder contained brine shrimp that hatched when mixed with water.
2   Tibor Kalman was a Hungarian graphic designer who cofounded the New York design studio M&Co and created iconic works like *Colors* magazine (supported by the Benetton clothing company) and music videos for the band the Talking Heads. Seymour Chwast cofounded Push Pin Studios, also in New York, with Milton Glaser and is still among the most prolific illustrators and artists working today.
3   Ghosting refers to the occurrence of multiple images appearing simultaneously as the angle at which the print is being viewed shifts.
4   It would have quadrupled the retail price.

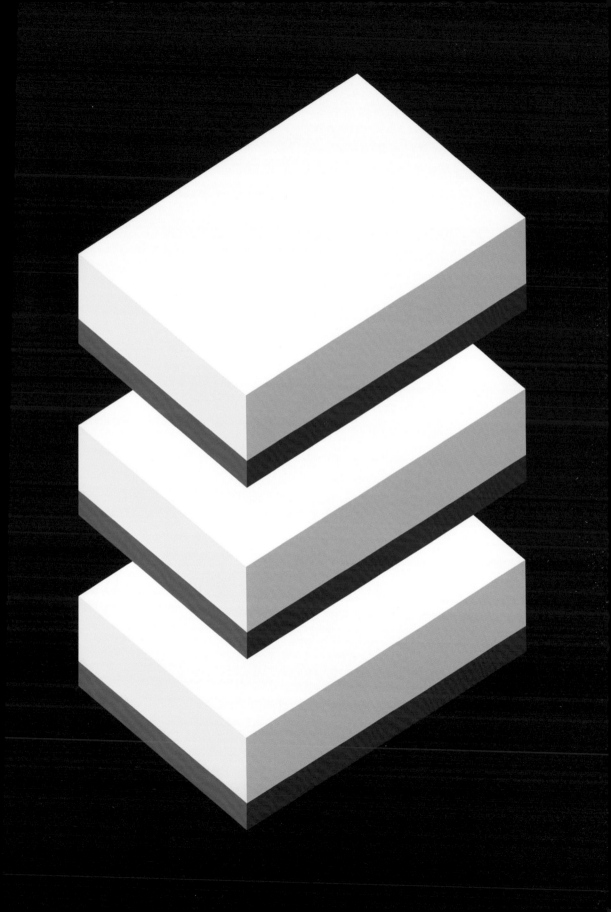

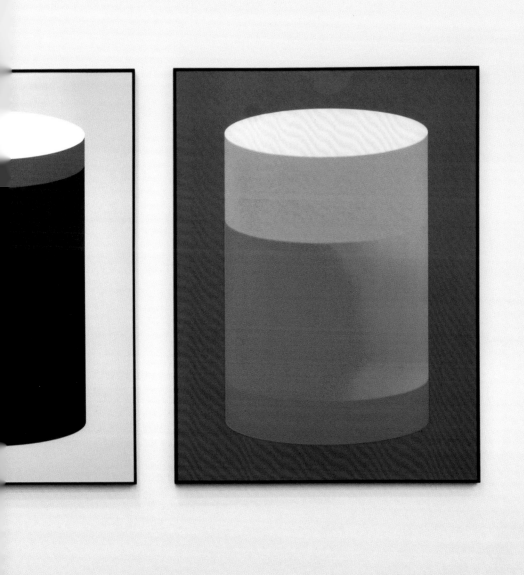

EMBROIDERING DATA. In 1999, the Chinese organization Tradition Now invited me to visit Suzhou, a 2,500-year-old Chinese settlement famous for its mastery of traditional crafts, to observe its woodcut printers, paper cutters, lantern makers, and embroiderers, and to discuss a possible collaboration. Situated just west of Shanghai on the Yangtze River, the city is known as one of the most livable in China.[1] Observing a master embroiderer there, I was immediately captivated by the process, as I had never worked in this technique before. The final embroidered pieces, created by five women working on a single area simultaneously, feature incredible detail and use hundreds of different colors. The results are almost photorealistic. A collaborative project was determined: I'd create three designs that their embroiderers would then

◄ ILLITERACY (detail)

Percentage of the world's population that is illiterate, 1820–2020. Created in collaboration with Yau Jiang Ping, Su Embroidery, China

execute in an edition of two (one set would be sent to me and they would keep the other set). Once completed, their set of the embroidered works would then be exhibited in October, thirteen months away.

Back home in New York, I received a message that the exhibition date has moved up to that coming October, reducing the time frame for design and by-hand production from thirteen months to just four weeks. Without the kind pleading of my friendly Chinese contact, Han, I certainly would have removed myself from the project.

A few days later, I sent them my designs for three large embroidered pieces and, by working day and night, they managed to get all three pieces embroidered in time to be exhibited during Suzhou Design Week.[2] The exhibited set was claimed by the local government, and lengthy negotiations became necessary for the second set to be created. The embroidery process had proven to be significantly more complex than anticipated, and the talented embroiderers who completed the first set were reluctant about having to do it all a second time. Ultimately, the second set was gorgeously executed by Yao Jianping of Su Embroidery in Suzhou and shared with me.

These pieces were among the very first data visualizations I designed within the *Now Is Better* series. I chose to depict elemental data sets relating to how illiteracy, homicide, and poverty have developed over the past two hundred years.

Details of embroidered works *Poverty* (left, center) and *Illiteracy* (right)

1   Feng Difan, "Suzhou, Beijing and Tianjin Rank as China's Most Livable Cities on EIU Global List," *Yicai Global*, August 15, 2018, www.yicaiglobal. com/news/suzhou-beijing-and-tianjin-rank-as-china-most-livable-cities-on-eiu-global-list.

2   This Suzhou Design Week took place October 2019 at the Suzhou Cultural Economy Exhibition and Exchange Center.

HOMICIDE ▶

Number of murders in Italy per 100,000 people, 1820–2020. Created in collaboration with Yau Jiang Ping, Su Embroidery, China

Pages 168–69: Installation view of the three embroidered works, Thomas Erben Gallery, New York, 2021 ▶▶

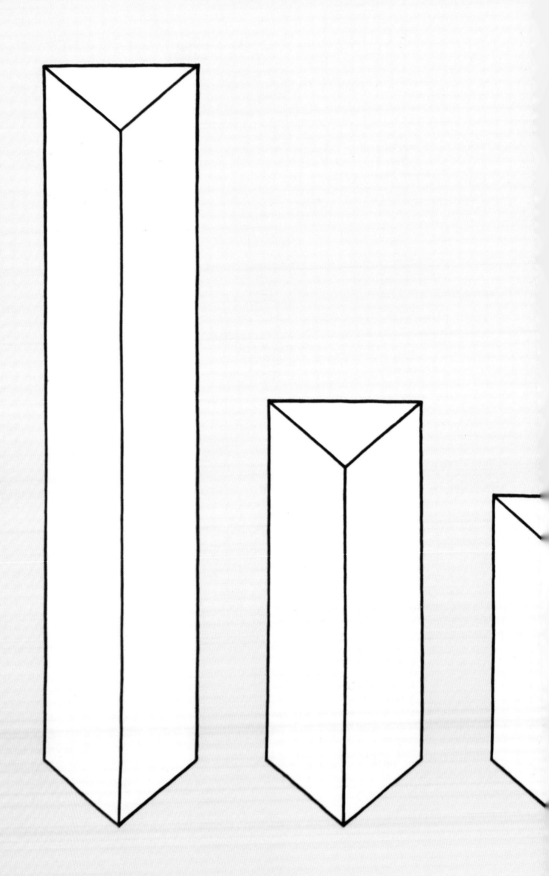

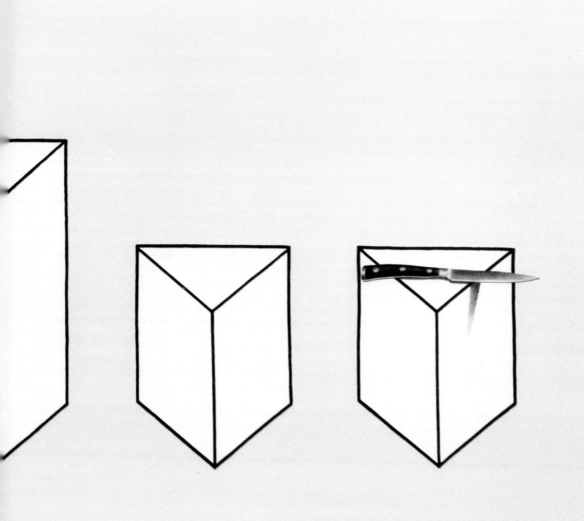

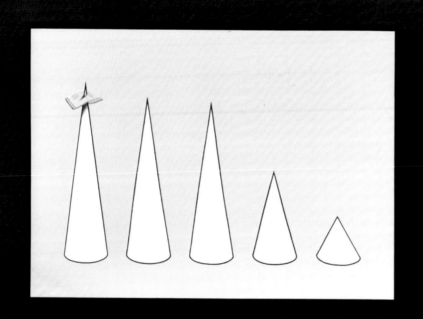
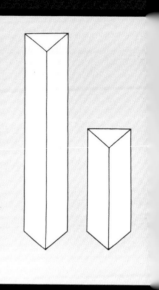

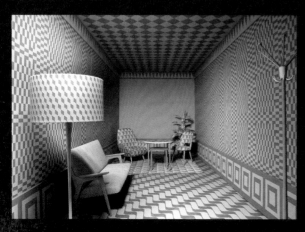

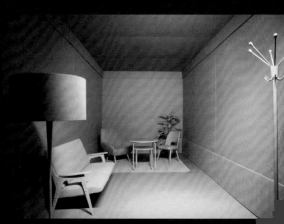

SELL THESE THINGS! *The Happy Show*—an exhibition about my own (un)happiness—traveled to ten museums around the world and attracted half a million visitors. *Beauty*, a show created together with Jessica Walsh, became the most visited show in the MAK Vienna's 150-year history. Nothing was for sale in these exhibitions, as the pieces shown were created solely to make a point, not to serve as decor. The *Now Is Better* exhibition was different. The central purpose of the work includes its installation in someone's home to serve as a reminder that the latest scandal or catastrophe does not necessarily mean the entire world is going downhill. If we sold nothing during the first exhibition at the Thomas Erben Gallery in New York, I would have declared it a failure and moved on. Luckily, we sold every painting.

◀ *First and second rows*: Installation views, *The Happy Show*, MAK Vienna, 2015
Third and fourth rows: Installation views, *Sagmeister & Walsh: Beauty*, MAK Vienna, 2018

Pages 172-177: Installation views, Thomas Erben Gallery, New York, 2021, and Museo Franz Mayer, Mexico City, 2022 ▶

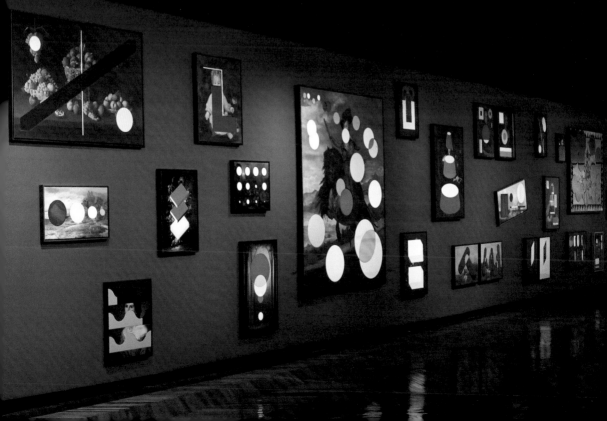

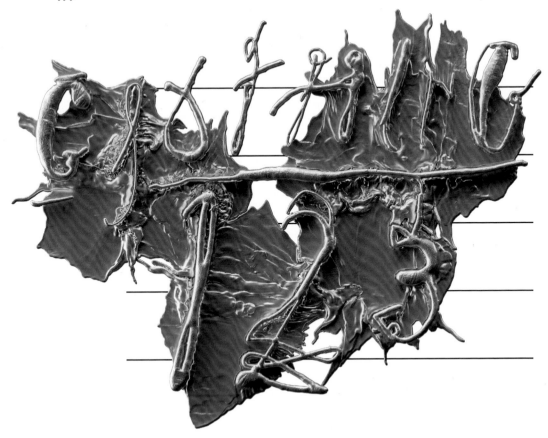

CLOTHING 123. My childhood home was located above my parents' clothing store in Bregenz, Austria, and predictably inspired within me a rebellion—an absolute disinterest in fashion. I preferred my older brothers' hand-me-downs to the new pieces sold in stores. It was only while working on the *Now Is Better* series that I began to imagine designing something wearable, something close to the skin of the audience.

I've always regarded fashion and jewelry as among the most challenging design disciplines. Their closeness to our bodies leads many consumers to stick to styles they're familiar with, making it difficult to introduce new directions and silhouettes for our time. If I want to design a garment that people will actually wear, true

◀ **MURDEROUS COAT**

Number of homicides in Europe per 100,000 people, 1400–2000

innovation might prove difficult. While it will get the attention of the high-fashion experts in the media, the consumer might not exhibit the same interest. Very few masters, like Issey Miyake and Alexander McQueen, found ways to walk that thin line successfully, and even in their cases, many of the runway pieces never went into production and were ultimately treated as works of art with a short life the length of a runway.

While tempted to establish a small fashion label, I had no desire to design within a seasonal schedule and zero interest in the creation of a system in need of constant feeding. In the end, we created twelve pieces: three t-shirts, three button-downs, two sweaters, a hoodie, a jacket, and two coats.[1]

The koala—one of the laziest animals in the forest—is the ideal logo for our clothing label

We might be called the laziest fashion company on the planet, with the term *slow fashion* taking on a whole new meaning. The perfect logo for such an endeavor proved to be the koala, one of the most laid-back animals of the wild. Constantly stoned from feeding on eucalyptus all day, the koala became our patron saint.

In keeping with the *lazy* concept, I did not design the koala logo myself but bought it ready-made from one of those cheap logo websites for two hundred dollars. My friend Santiago's company, Art Camp, beautifully animated the logo to make it come alive.

As for the name of the brand itself, the *laziest* version I could think of was Sagmeister123. My partner, Karolina, agreed to design the online store, and my former partner, Anni, produced the garments. My nephew Clemens and

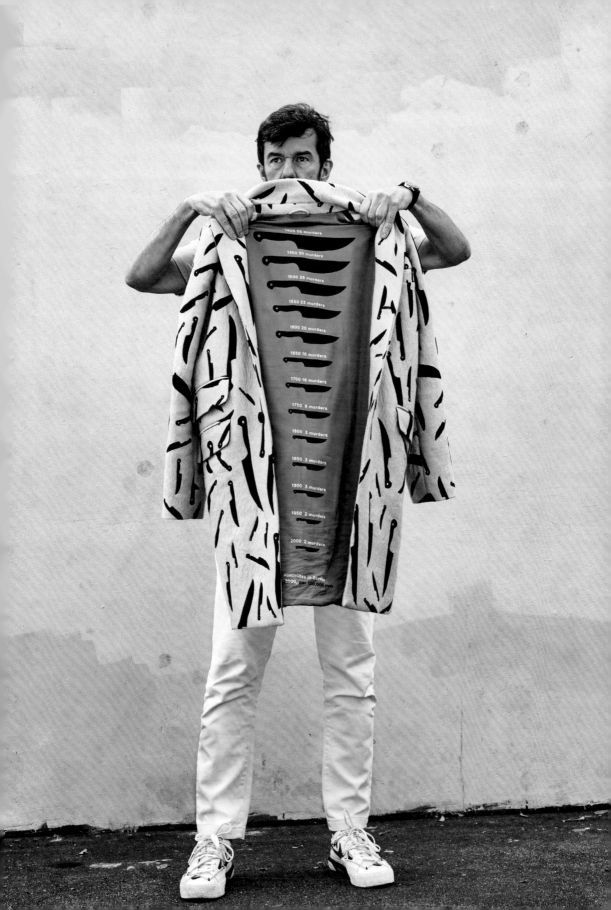

1400 55 murders
1450 30 murders
1500 25 murders
1550 23 murders
1600 20 murders
1650 16 murders
1700 16 murders
1750 8 murders
1800 3 murders
1850 3 murders
1900 3 murders
1950 2 murders
2000 2 murders

Homicides in Europe
2000 per 100,000 ppts

sister-in-law Susanne agreed to sell the clothes in their stores, making the entire operation a true family affair.

In order for Anni to directly converse with those who printed, cut, and sewed the garments, we decided to produce everything locally in New York. Sadly, this also meant that the retail prices would be quite high.

Besides the pleasure of being able to walk around in my own garments,[2] I also found out how complex the design and production of clothing really is, gaining new respect for the profession.

◀ OPINION COAT ▶

Percentage of people in the
United States who believe
that women should return to
their traditional roles in society,
1910–2010

1 Later on, we added another five pieces: three
   t-shirts, a winter coat, and another sweater.
2 An often repeated exchange on the street:
   "I love your coat! Who designed it?" "I did."
   (with disbelief) "YOU did?" "Yes, I did."

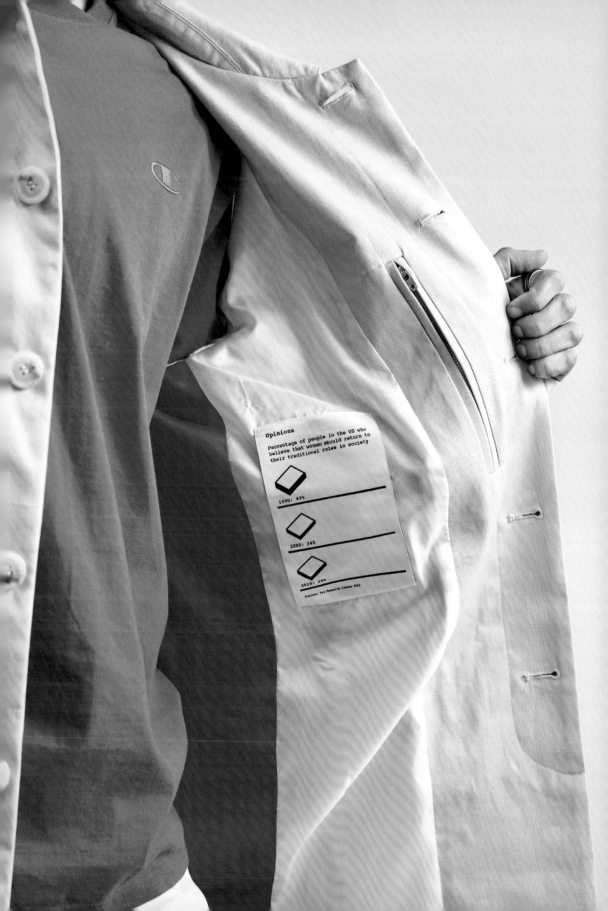

Opinions

Percentage of people in the US who
believe that women should return to
their traditional roles in society

1990: 49%

2000: 34%

2010: 25%

Source: Pew Research Center 2012

QUAKES, FLOODS, HURRICANES

Number of deaths worldwide as a result of natural disasters, 1920–1930 vs. 2010–2020, visualized in a historical painting and on a long-sleeved t-shirt

LIFE

Average global life expectancy,
1800 vs. 2020, visualized on a dress
shirt and in a historical canvas

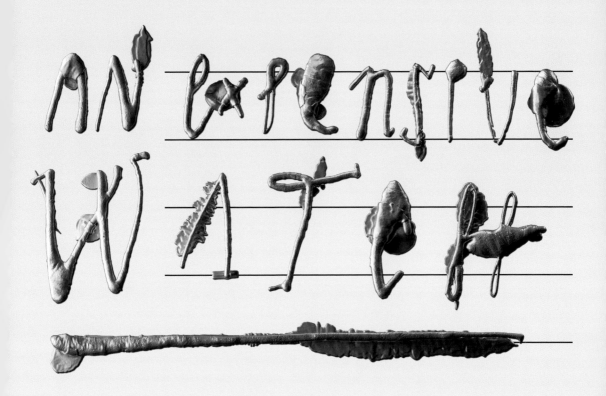

AN EXPENSIVE WATCH. The bookstores in the Zurich airport carry an annual magazine that contains an image of every single watch manufactured in Switzerland that year. After a family visit, I often pick up one of these hefty tomes, enjoying a soothing leaf through on the plane ride home to New York.

For several consecutive years, my favorite design in the publication was created for the Ressence brand: a fully mechanical watch that replaces the traditional minute and hour hands with discs turning against and within each other. The results are conceptually amazing and very aesthetically pleasing. I continue to be impressed by the obsessiveness of the designer, who went to considerable trouble to reinvent the interface of the mechanical watch in an age when digital and smart versions are taking over the industry.

THIS SUM AIN'T ZERO

Trade Openness Index (the sum
of all world exports and imports,
as a share of the world's GDP),
1917 vs. 2017

I've always looked at expensive watches critically. From a functional point of view, products like the Apple Watch are clearly superior to even the most complicated mechanical timepiece.[1] Nevertheless, I fell under the spell, and years later purchased a blue Ressence Type 1.

I wrote a congratulatory note to the watch's designer, Benoît Mintiens, thanking him for his vision. A year later, Benoît contacted me with an offer to possibly design a limited-edition version of the Type 3X watch, similar to the Type 1 model

Ressence Type 3X watch, 2021, edition of 40

except that the upper half is filled with oil. He proposed a deal in which I'd receive the first watch in exchange for my design services. But of course! The design process proved to be straightforward, and thankfully the most challenging mechanical work had already been engineered by Benoît. I had wanted to replace the date ring on the outside of the dial with thin, alternating blue and orange bars. This, I thought, would be achievable by printing a black mask with narrow strip-like openings on the *inside* of the crystal glass watch face, which would allow the blue and orange bits of the date dial to shine through and give the watch a different colored ring on alternating days.

This would have worked if not for the fact that the number thirty-one (from the monthly date dial) is a prime number and prevented the math from resolving neatly. I was ready to go back to the drawing board when Benoît came up with a solution involving the design of special internal cogs to overcome the mathematical difficulties.

Every single line on the face of the watch was cut into

its surface using a CNC router, then individually filled in by hand using a tiny paintbrush. The same painstaking process was repeated for the color used to denote nighttime, which glows in the dark.

The edition of forty sold out on the first day.

---

1 I might also argue that the team responsible for the Apple Watch, including Jony Ive and Marc Newson, is simply more talented than almost anybody working for a Swiss luxury brand today.

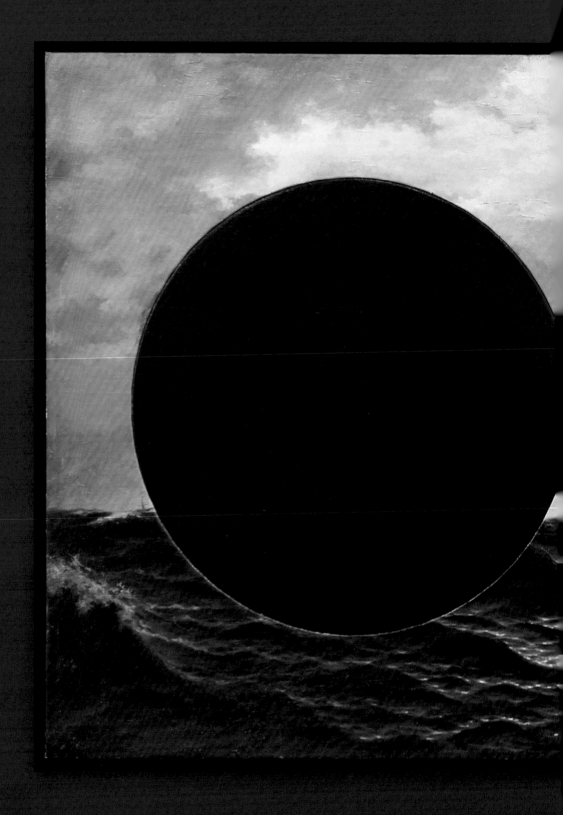

COFFEE AND WATER. I usually enjoy about ten cups of espresso each day, making the espresso cup one of the most important mainstays in my house. Given this, it made sense to design cups bearing the *Now Is Better* message. I wanted to employ a somewhat abstract visual strategy, fearing that an overtly direct message might get stale over time. I've never enjoyed jokey or message-driven coffee cups ("World's Best Boss" comes to mind).

When the Italian coffee brand Illy offered me the opportunity to design cups within their famed artist series—a roster including David Byrne, Jeff Koons, and Louise Bourgeois—I immediately jumped at the chance. The shape of the cup itself had been created by Matteo Thun, an Italian architect and designer who taught product design at the University of Applied

◀ Lobmeyr glassware, 2022
(top to bottom, left to right):
Health & Sickness,
1820 vs. 2020;
Life & Death, 1820 vs. 2019;
Knowledge & Ignorance,
1820–2016;
Democracy & Dictatorship,
1820–2016;
Food & Hunger, 1820–2015;
Peace & War, 1795–2015

Arts in Vienna during my time there. The design *on* the cup, however, was entirely open for my interpretation.

Anamorphic images have long held a special fascination for me. It's a technique that originated in the Ming dynasty in China and was later utilized in seventeenth-century Europe to conceal an image through distortion, its true nature only revealed with the aid of a cylindrical mirror.[1]

We created the cylindrical mirror by covering the existing cup in chrome and designed colorful graphics for the saucer.

When reflected into the mirrored cup, these graphics reveal themselves as data visualizations. The six cups illustrate six different ways in which the world has improved over the past century, from the rising number of democratic countries to increasing female representation in government.

Besides espresso, I consume copious amounts of sparkling water. The most beautiful water glasses I know of are created by the venerable manufacturer J. & L. Lobmeyr in Vienna.[2] We had collaborated with them previously, and their individually hand-painted glasses seemed perfect for the *Now Is Better* series.

The colorful design of the saucer is reflected in the mirrored cup as a data visualization

While traveling in Central America, I designed a series of eight glasses, each illustrated with various types of tropical leaves. Doubling as data visualizations, the leaves depict issues concerning the environment that have shown positive change over time. This includes the global expansion of protected sites with great biodiversity as well as the increasing number of countries who have signed the Kyoto Protocol and the United Nations Framework Convention on Climate Change treaty.[3] Each glass is painted by hand twice: from the front, you'll see the top of the leaf, and looking at the back of the glass, you'll see the underside of each leaf, painted separately.

An espresso cup from the Illy Art Collection

Since this highly realistic hand painting resulted in high retail prices, I also wanted to create a (somewhat) more afford-able version. In a second series of glasses (also with J. & L. Lobmeyr), we reduced the design to minimalistic circles, etched into the glass using a simple grinding wheel. We selected six classic data sets, collected over the past two hundred years, that respectively illustrate how the poverty rate, life expectancy, health, literacy, democracy, and times of peace have been improved and elongated since the early 1800s.

1   J. L. Hunt, B. G. Nickel, and Christian Gigault, "Anamorphic Images," *American Journal of Physics* 68, no. 232 (2000).
2   J. & L. Lobmeyr not only created the chandelier for the Schoenbrunn Palace but also developed the world's first electrical chandelier for Thomas Edison. "J. and L. Lobmeyr," *Cooper-Hewitt,*

Smithsonian Design Museum, www.collection. cooperhewitt.org/people/18045401.
3   The Kyoto Protocol is a treaty that commits states to reducing greenhouse gas emissions. The UN Framework Convention on Climate Change is an international treaty to combat "dangerous human interference with the climate system."

Amount of stuff
used by the average person in the UK per year:

top: 2001 15 tons
bottom: 2013 10 tons

Greenhouse gases are caused by:

clockwise from bottom left:
Live stock: 5.5%
Energy: 13%
Deforestation: 15%
Industry: 29%
Buildings: 18%
Transport: 16.5%
Various others: 3%

Percentage of worldwide marine protected a

top: 2016 9%
bottom: 2017 11.5%

GREEN CLIMATE FUND

SIGNED PLEDGES

US   3
UK   1.2
FRANCE 1.0
GERM   1.0
SPAIN 0.5
S KOREA 0.25
SWEDEN 0.1
AUSTRIA 0.03

total 7 TRILLION TOTAL

Number of countries who signed the UN Climate Change Convention:

top left: 2000 184 countries
top right: 2003 187 countries
mid left: 2006 188 countries
mid right: 2009 193 countries
bottom left: 2012 195 countries
bottom right: 2015 197 countries

Number of countries who signed the Kyoto Protocol:

From left to right:
2000: 31 countries
2005: 157 countries
2010: 192 countries
2015: 193 countries

Percentage of world population without access to clean water:

From top to bottom:
1990: 25%
1995: 21%
2000: 18%
2005: 15%
2010: 12%
2015: 9%

BACK OF LE

Lobmeyr glassware, 2021
(left to right):
*Percentage of marine
protected areas around the
world, 2016 vs. 2017;*
*Number of countries who
signed the Paris Agreement
of the UN Climate Change
Convention, 2000–2015;*
*Monetary pledges to the
Green Climate Fund, various
countries, 2018;*
*Amount of stuff consumed
yearly per average person
in the United Kingdom,
2001 vs. 2013;*
*Percentage of important global
biodiversity sites that are
environmentally protected,
2000–2018;*
*Percentage of world population
without access to clean water,
1990–2015*

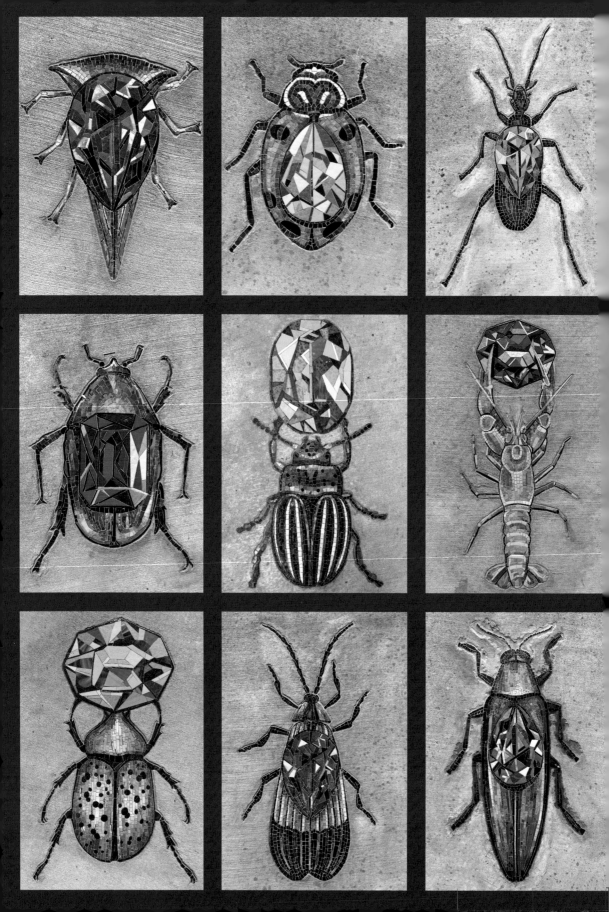

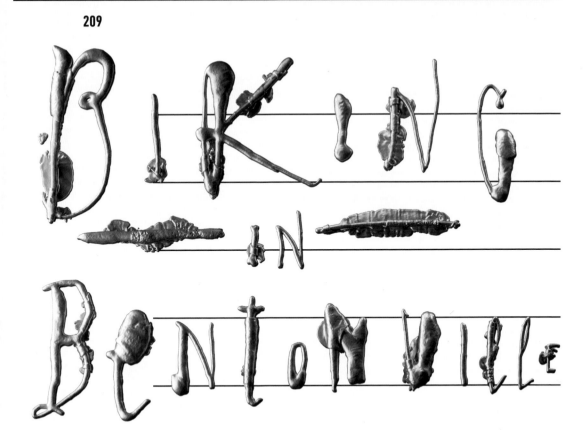

BIKING IN BENTONVILLE. In the Ozark Mountains in northern Arkansas, the town of Bentonville is destined to become the mountain bike capital of the United States. Situated along winding rivers and never-ending forests, dozens of bike paths have been thoughtfully constructed. It therefore made perfect sense for the town's Ledger office building—designed by my friend Michel Rojkind—to provide people the option to bike right up to their offices, thanks to a seven-floor wraparound ramp. Upon its construction, I was asked to design the ramp and visited Arkansas to get a better sense of the project. Bentonville is a pretty town with excellent restaurants and sophisticated murals as well as the Crystal Bridges Museum of American Art and the Momentary, an art gallery exhibiting contemporary work. We were

◀ **NOW IS BETTER**

Glass mosaics set in concrete at the Ledger office building in Bentonville, Arkansas

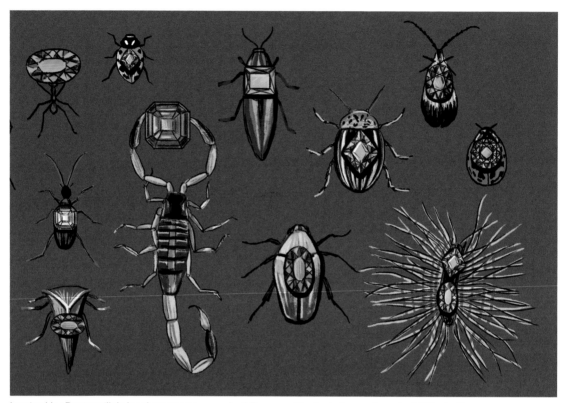

Inspired by Bentonville's local creatures, we asked Raxenne Maniquiz to create colorful illustrations

shown the surrounding hills and valleys from a small plane and explored the wide network of custom-built paths on electric mountain bikes, riding past gurgling rivers and stunning waterfalls.

The design brief stated that the ramp design did not need to be too closely tied to wayfinding, but should allow for a more open design interpretation that featured something unique to the Ozarks.

We selected creatures native to the area, with illustrator Raxenne Maniquiz drawing each one. The illustrations were then laid out as glass mosaics by Franz Mayer of Munich, a company founded in 1847 that had once created stained-glass windows and mosaics for the Bavarian king.

These illustrations were then transformed into mosaics by Franz Mayer of Munich

Having worked most of my life in ephemeral media, it's satisfying to imagine these mosaics being around for a long time. During a recent visit to Italian city of Ravenna, I admired mosaics from the year 850. They are still in excellent shape more than one thousand years later.

Today, more than one hundred critters appear to be carrying gemstones along the ramp up toward the building's rooftop terrace, where the stones are neatly deposited to form my favorite phrase: Now Is Better.

Critters, created in mosaic and set flush into the concrete bike path, carrying precious stones to the rooftop of the Ledger office building in Bentonville, Arkansas ▶

Mosaic, titled *Now Is Better*, on the top floor of the Ledger office building in Bentonville, Arkansas ▶▶

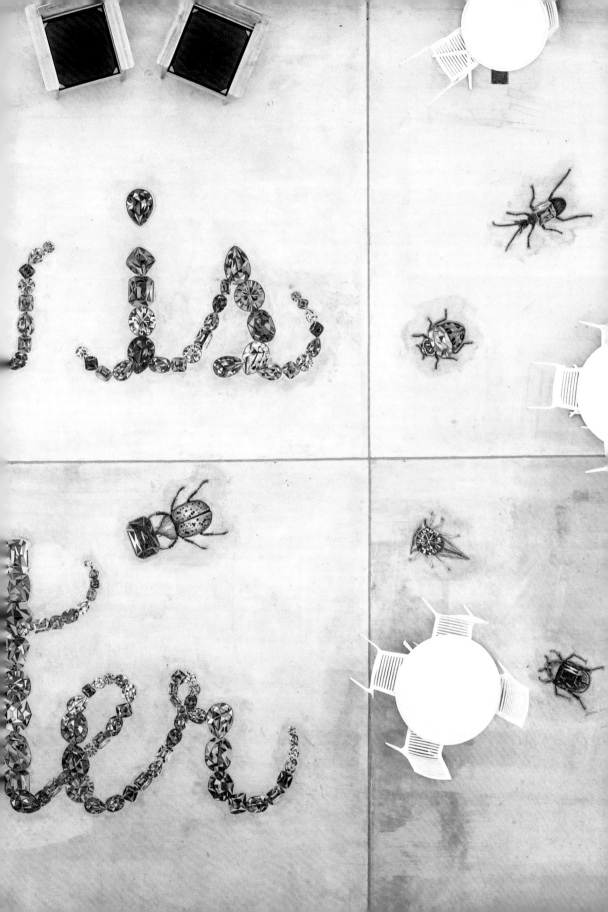

NUMBER OF VISITORS TO Concerts

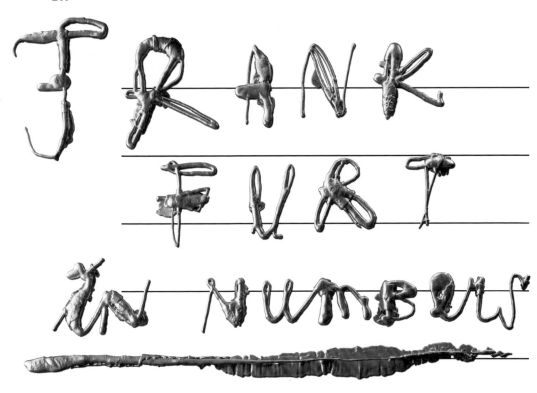

FRANKFURT IN NUMBERS. When the pharmaceutical giant Bayer outgrew its Frankfurt headquarters, its mid-century modern office building was transformed into a hotel in 2008. Originally designed by Stefan Blattner in 1952, the building features a proper paternoster—a doorless elevator in constant motion that you have to jump into at the opportune opening—as well as a grand restaurant on the top floor overlooking the city.

This hotel was my home during the installation of *Beauty* at the Museum for Applied Arts in Frankfurt. At the time, the hotel's director was commissioning large murals for the lobby and courtyard. We in turn commissioned the research department of the *Frankfurter Allgemeine Zeitung* (Frankfurt's best newspaper, in my opinion) to seek out data relating to the advancement of

◀ *Opposite* and *page 218*: Number of visitors to concerts in Frankfurt since 1950 (detail). Hand-painted mural, Flemings Hotel, Frankfurt, Germany

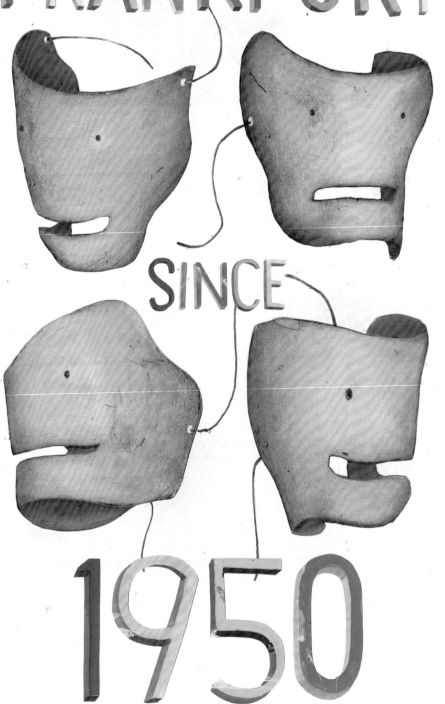

Number of ice cream parlors in Frankfurt
since 1950 (in-progress)

various local developments in the past seventy years. How
did theaters and performance spaces develop? How about ice
cream parlors? Are there as many such spaces today as before?

While the pandemic and a change in leadership resulted
in a scaling back of the project, a number of our designs were
executed, illustrated by artist Jason Holley.

Number of ice cream parlors
in Frankfurt since 1950 (detail).
Hand-painted mural, Flemings
Hotel, Frankfurt, Germany ▶

ARLORS

SINCE 1950

Interview: Hans Ulrich Obrist & Stefan Sagmeister

HANS ULRICH OBRIST:
Hello, hello! Are you in New York right now?

STEFAN SAGMEISTER:
Yes. I've been based in New York for the past thirty years.

HANS ULRICH:
Are there other places where you spend time?

STEFAN:
New York is the place I've lived the longest, but I worked in Hong Kong for two years and was in Bali for a year and a half.

◀ EVE

Collective harvest of the world's apples, 1962–2017

HANS ULRICH:
What brought you to Indonesia?

STEFAN:
I conduct a sabbatical every seven years, shutting down the studio for one year. In 2000, I spent the first sabbatical in New York, so seven years later, I wanted to change it up for the second. Indonesia has gorgeous landscapes and kind people, and its craft scene was enticing.

HANS ULRICH:
Philippe Parreno and Pierre Huyghe once started an association to liberate time.

STEFAN:
It's proved to be a great strategy to gain perspective on what I'm doing. These years are also instrumental in being able to see my work not just as a job but also as a calling.

HANS ULRICH:
365 days is a long time. What do you do during the sabbaticals?

STEFAN:
In the beginning of the first sabbatical, I had purposefully made no plans. This didn't turn out well, as I wound up occupying myself with busywork, like sending files to Japanese design magazines who requested them.

I needed a plan. I made a list of all the things I was interested in, then scheduled five weekly hours for large-scale design directions I was truly excited by and one hour for smaller projects, resulting in a grade school-like schedule: Monday, 9 a.m. to noon working on typographic comics, noon to 2 p.m. writing, and so on. After a couple of months, many projects were up and running and I could throw out the schedule.

HANS ULRICH:
During your most recent sabbatical, what did you study?

STEFAN:
I spent time in three different locations: Mexico City, Tokyo, and Schwarzenberg, in the Austrian Alps. The big, overall subject was beauty. I used to think of myself as a conceptual designer, unconcerned about style or form. But through experience, I found that whenever we take form and aesthetics seriously, the pieces seem to function better. I wanted to explore this.

Ultimately, the year yielded a large exhibition on beauty, created together with Jessica Walsh, that opened at the Museum of Applied Arts in Vienna (MAK) and traveled to four more museums. It attracted the most visitors in the history of the MAK.

HANS ULRICH:
What prompted the *Now Is Better* project? How did it begin?

HIGH AND LOW ▶

Average life expectancy at birth in the United Kingdom, 1700 vs. 2020

STEFAN:

I was a resident at the American Academy in Rome in 2019 and was sitting one night next to the husband of one of the artists at dinner. This highly educated lawyer told me that what we are seeing right now in Hungary, Poland, and Brazil signifies the end of modern democracy.[1]

After dinner, I Googled the historical development of modern democracy and found that two hundred years ago, only one democratic country existed. Today, ninety-six countries qualify as democratic, and for the first time in history, more than half of humanity lives within a democratic system.[2]

I found the phenomenon of a highly educated person, so influenced by the daily news cycle that he carries a completely wrong view of the world, fascinating. From a communication-design point of view, it seemed an interesting direction to tackle.

HANS ULRICH:

I often speak with Brian Eno, who told me about his collaboration on the Long Now Foundation with Stewart Brand and Daniel Hillis.[3] And there has been a very interesting book by Roman Krznaric about the question of how to be a good ancestor and how we can liberate society from short-termism.[4]

◀ ACCIDENTS

Yearly fatal occupational accidents in the United States per 100,000 workers, 1910–2010

STEFAN:

Daniel Hillis, Stewart Brand, and Brian Eno are certainly among the brightest people I've ever met in my life.

HANS ULRICH:

This opens up the possibility to work on projects that take longer to finish, or maybe never finish. Antoni Gaudí's Sagrada Família is an example.

STEFAN:

Yes! The golden wall, called Pala d'Oro, in Saint Mark's Basilica in Venice is another one. Its construction began around 950 and was completed nearly four hundred years later.

As a designer, I am very much used to ephemeral work. When we design a website, it might be changed the next day. A poster may be up for a couple of weeks. I had hopes for longevity when we designed album covers, but ultimately, they were thrown out when the CD ceased to be a dominant format.

For the *Now Is Better* project, I looked for a medium that I could reasonably expect to be around for a while. I chose historic oil paintings, as they had already survived two or three centuries, and I assume they'll last for another good stretch of time. From a conceptual point of view, it makes sense to visualize long-term data through a long-term medium.

On some subjects, like war, we can capture long-term data going back seven hundred years. On matters like the tone of the news, the time span would be significantly shorter, but we can still gather reliable data for a fifty-year period.

HANS ULRICH:

You started the *Now Is Better* series during the lockdown, surrounded by short-term media and Zoom conversations.

You began to look at data. You then allowed this data to migrate through various media: painting, embroidered canvases, different printing techniques. There is also the very pre-digital, handmade quality of these works. Can you talk a little bit about where the data is from and how it gets transformed into these different media?

STEFAN:

I collect data from scientific sources I trust. This could be Steven Pinker's research at Harvard, or Max Roser, a German scientist at Oxford who runs Our World in Data. I'm a member of Statista. And of course, Hans and Ola Rosling have been able to wrangle a lot of data from various institutions for their Ignorance Project.

I tend to concentrate on counterintuitive data about human progress developing well. Many of my friends find this data hard to believe, which is why I always include source information.

As mentioned, I try to use media that will be around for a long time. The hand-painted glasses we designed for Lobmeyr in Vienna are expensive, and hopefully beautiful, so they won't be thrown out quickly. They are created by utilizing an extremely slow technique.[5] And they live in somebody's home, at the center of their dining table. When you drink out of such a glass, you're reminded that certain things develop positively in the long term.

The same is true for the mechanical watch we designed for Ressence. It's not a fashion watch you'd set aside for the latest trends, and it can be expected to be around for many decades.

ESSERE SOCIALE ▶

Percentage of GDP spent on social programs in Italy, 1930–2010

HANS ULRICH:

Participation plays a big role in your work. You once said you were inspired by the salons of Louise Bourgeois, which I also attended. Twelve people would meet in her living room and everybody had to bring their work, which she then critiqued in a rather fierce way. Can you talk about how Bourgeois inspired you? And about how this project is participatory?

STEFAN:

That was a seminal experience. She was very tough and also extremely generous. I brought my first book, *Made You Look*, which she appreciated. She started dictating the names of various people to me that I was supposed to visit. After a second she asked, "Well actually, do you want to become an artist?" And I said, "I'm quite happy being a designer." That concluded her interest in me.

There was a woman who had traveled from Japan for an opportunity to meet her idol. She carefully unwrapped her work, which turned out to be chocolate hands that she had cast. Louise circled the table, not saying anything for two long minutes, stopped, looked at the Japanese artist and cried: "Why are you doing these things?" It was radical.

The experience prompted me to copy Bourgeois's idea, and for many years we put on salon-like events on Monday evenings in the studio, during which young designers could come in and I would review their work.

I ultimately shifted these critiques online, to Instagram, where I'm still doing them today. I review a piece from a young designer every day.[6] This way, the audience can be much, much larger, but of course you can't be that harsh on Instagram, and the critique tends to be a bit shallower than an in-person review.

As far as the participatory nature of these pieces is concerned, these connections usually occur once they are sold; I am in contact with some of the collectors who bought paintings at Thomas Erben Gallery in Chelsea.[7] Because of the unusual combination of contemporary inserts and historic paintings, the pieces prompt questions from visitors to the collectors' homes, beginning interesting conversations.

That is the ideal outcome. It's what made me create this series.

This interview took place over Zoom on Sept. 9, 2022.

1 Populist right-wing governments had recently been elected in these countries, curtailing certain democratic principles.

2 "Distribution of Democracy," *Our World in Data*, 2018, www.ourworldindata.org/grapher/distribution-democracy-polity.

3 Brian Eno has helped shape the ambient music genre and also works as a visual artist. Stewart Brand created and edited the *Whole Earth Catalog* and the WELL. Brand is also co-founder of the Long Now Foundation, along with Danny Hillis, a US computer scientist and inventor who pioneered paralell computers and their use in artificial intelligence.

4 Roman Krznaric is a philosopher from Australia.

5 The glasses are hand-painted twice, so that the top of the leaf shows when viewed from one side of the glass and the bottom of the leaf shows from the other side (see pages 200–207).

6 To see these reviews, head to @stefansagmeister on Instagram.

7 We sold all the paintings.

PRECEDENTS ▶

Deaths as a result of global pandemics over the past 200 years

THE TUNNELS IN TORONTO. Camilla Dalglish's daughter had fallen seriously ill and was spending a lot of time in the hospital. Wheeled through a tunnel connecting the five major hospitals in Toronto, her nurse pushed her gurney past a maze of decommissioned hospital beds and medical waste dumpsters. This decaying concrete system of tunnels served as the path for many patients being transported to different hospitals for procedures or doctors' visits, which are a cause for anxiety in and of themselves.

Having experienced this environment during her daughter's illness, Dalglish decided to act. She and the University Health Network persuaded all five Toronto hospitals to work together to not only improve the dreary underground infrastructure but also to beautify it. Dalglish and the Weston Family Foundation raised

◀ *Tunnels in Toronto*, a mural connecting the five major hospitals of Toronto. Detail of illustration by Linus Lohoff

Before

money for a redesign and, after a complex search, commissioned us for the task.

Considering the half-mile total length of the tunnels and the budget allotted, it became clear that we could not address larger structural issues and would have to make improvements using only paint, light, and sound. Through the *Beauty* exhibition, I had become friends with Viennese scientist Helmut Leder, who is known for his research regarding the psychological processes involved in the appreciation of art and aesthetics. He prompted one of his graduate students to gather scientific research that explored the relationship between design and healing.

While all reports supported the general notion of the physical environment affecting the well-being of patients in a medical setting, I was surprised that most studies ended with sentences like:

After

- On the basis of the available research, it would be premature to formulate evidence-based guidelines for designing health care environments.
- The field thus appears to be in urgent need of well-conducted, controlled clinical trials.
- When scrutinizing the effects of specific environmental stimuli, conclusive evidence is still very limited and difficult to generalize.

It became clear that the original brief, specifying that the design program should promote *healing*, was not possible. People do not simply get better by being pushed through a concrete tunnel, no matter how well-designed this tunnel may be.

We settled on *calming* as our guiding theme. One constant thread that emerged from the three dozen research papers

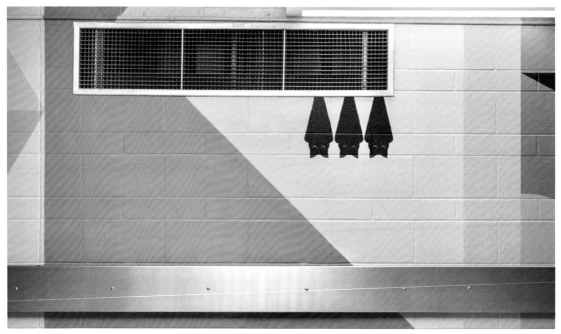

We tried to incorporate preexisting architectural elements…

consulted was the idea that visuals from nature seem to register a measurable positive effect on patients. Considering the stress and anxiety inherent in this environment, the studies agreed that images in and around hospitals should feature unambiguously positive subject matter.

Working closely with Barcelona-based designer Linus Lohoff, we created a color palette inspired by the flora and fauna of Canada, featuring lots of muted blues, earthy ochres, and piney greens. We tried to create designs that struck a balance between realistic nature illustrations and pure abstraction, purposefully including recognizable forms like flowers, birds, and butterflies though leaving them open-ended enough to let one's mind wander beyond the tunnel walls.

Besides transporting patients from one facility to another, the hospitals also utilize these tunnels for storage. Much of the walls and ceilings are cluttered with pipes, emergency boxes,

...into our designs.

and electrical cabinets. Successfully negotiating the elimination
of all these elements—considering the involvement of five
different hospital bureaucracies—seemed impossible. So, we
decided to embrace these conditions and use them as the
starting point for our designs: birds wound up chirping from
electrical boxes, and spiders descended on strings from steam
pipes. We also incorporated Dalglish's idea of a repeating design
element that encourages an adult to prompt a child to seek
out and count, such as: "How many blue birds can you see?"

The tunnels opened in the fall of 2022. As this project was
created during the COVID-19 pandemic within a health care
environment, lots of difficulties arose, but they were brilliantly
overcome by our on-site producer, Nigel Scott of Devil's Thumb.
The music for the tunnels was written and performed on
piano by Victoria Hong, one of the patients in the clinic at the
University Health Network.

The murals connecting the five major hospitals of Toronto span...

...more than half of a mile (800 meters).

MOVE OUR MONEY. More than twenty years ago, and long before the *Now Is Better* series, philanthropist and Ben & Jerry's cofounder Ben Cohen commissioned a group of large-scale data visualizations from us. Having achieved considerable influence as a business owner and activist, he assembled roughly two hundred business leaders, CEOs, and military advisers—including corporate celebrities like Ted Turner, founder of the Cable News Network (CNN), and Paul Newman, actor and founder of the brand Newman's Own—under the banner of Move Our Money.

The Move Our Money group created a program titled "Business Leaders for Sensible Priorities," which advocated for the reduction of the Pentagon's budget by 15 percent and reallocating this amount to health care and educational programs.[1] They planned to achieve this

◀ **MOVE OUR MONEY**

Enamel pin visualizing the United States discretionary budget, 1999

"Global Military Spending" inflates into a three-dimensional bar chart, revealing the United States and its allies far outspending all other countries

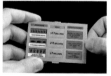

Move Our Money
slide card

without affecting the strength of the US military but by reducing unnecessary weapons programs and Pentagon waste.[2]
I was particularly enthusiastic about this initiative, as it was run by leadership from the business world and the military-industrial complex—rather than the usual leftist activists—who had real expertise to weigh in on the issue. Their stance was anti-waste, not anti-military.

Instead of a formal logo, we designed simplified charts illustrating the Pentagon's astronomical budget, which was $750 billion in 2021.[3] The most frequently used visual was a pie chart of the discretionary budget of the United States, as determined by Congress.[4] Half of that fund is spent on the military.

At the time of the project, I wore this logo as an enamel pin. I was asked countless times about its meaning, which gave me the chance to explain the program. As part of a traveling road show, some of the charts were designed as inflatable sculptures.

Volunteers drove an inverted double-decker school bus all around the United States. Due to its unusual shape, the bus

Volunteers driving the Topsy-Turvy Bus across the United States, 1999

wound up on local television—with these segments including the anchor reporting on the initiative—and generated considerable media coverage.

After a ten-year campaign, we found success in 2010, when President Barack Obama implemented significant parts of our program. In 2016, Trump reversed them.

1   The budget of the Pentagon (the headquarters of the US Department of Defense) funds the nation's six branches of military: Army, Navy, Marine Corps, Air Force, Coast Guard, and Space Force.
2   Pentagon "waste" refers to the purchase of weapons systems that are either unworkable or unnecessary.
3   "Yes, Pentagon's Annual Budget Is Twice the Spending Proposed to Pay for Build Back Better Act," *Politifact*, www.politifact.com/factchecks/2021/oct/14/mark-pocan/yes-pentagons-annual-budget-twice-spending-propose.
4   Federal spending is classified as either mandatory or discretionary. About 63 percent of the federal budget is mandatory spending, 30 percent is discretionary spending, and the rest is interest payments on debt.

Regarding all historical paintings in the *Now Is Better* series: The foundational canvases were originally painted in the seventeenth, eighteenth, or nineteenth century, the medium being oil on canvas or wood. They are now mounted on Masonite with contemporary inlays. All works in this series were created between 2019 and 2023. Photographs by Phillip Reed and Andreas Vesterlund.

FRONT COVER, PAGE 16
HER MARK
44 ¾ × 35 in. (114 × 89 cm)
Universal voting rights for women, 1916–2017 (top to bottom):
1916: 6%
1930: 30%
2017: 98%

Source: Bastien Herre, "Universal Right to Vote for Women," *Our World in Data*, 2021, www.ourworldindata.org

PAGE 6
WOMAN II
23 ⅝ × 20 ⅛ in. (60 × 51 cm)
Percentage of countries with at least one female member of parliament, 1920–2020:
1920: 2% (purple)
1970: 68% (yellow)
2020: 98% (blue)

Source: "Proportion of Seats Held by Women in National Parliaments," *Our World in Data*, 2022, www.ourworldindata.org/human-rights.

PAGE 9
MURDER
32 ⅝ × 21 ¼ in. (83 × 54 cm)
Homicides in Europe per 100,000 people, 1400–2000:
1400: 35% (red)
1600: 15% (pink)
1800: 3% (blue)
2000: 2% (yellow)

Source: Pieter Spierenburg, *A History of Murder: Personal Violence in Europe from the Middle Ages to the Present*, Cambridge, UK: Polity, 2008.

PAGE 13
WOMAN I
19 ⅝ × 17 in. (50 × 43 cm)
Percentage of countries in which women have the right to vote, 1900–2000:
1900: 0% (yellow)
1950: 65% (purple)
2000: 97% (blue)

Source: Bastien Herre, "Universal Right to Vote for Women," *Our World in Data*, 2021.

PAGE 14
LITERACY I
20 ⅞ × 16 1/4 in. (53 × 41 cm)
Percentage of people who can read and write, 1900–2000:
1900: 19% (purple)
1950: 58% (dark blue)
2000: 81% (light blue)

Source: Max Roser and Esteban Ortiz-Ospina, "Literacy," *Our World in Data*, 2016, www.ourworldindata.org/literacy.

PAGE 19
RICHER AND POORER
29 × 24 ⅛ in. (74 × 61 cm)
Top row: Percentage of the global population living in poverty, 1990–2020 (left to right):
1990: 35%
2005: 25%
2020: 9%
Bottom row: Results of a 2020 survey in which people shared their thoughts on the global poverty rate in the last thirty years (left to right):
12% believe the global poverty rate has improved
33% believe the global poverty rate has stayed the same
55% believe the global poverty rate has worsened

Source: Hans Rosling, "Highlights from Ignorance Survey in the UK," *Gapminder*, 2013, www.gapminder.org/news/highlights-from-ignorance-survey-in-the-uk.

PAGES 20 (DETAIL), 22
THESE SELF-EVIDENT TRUTHS
80 × 77 in. (203 × 196 cm)
Number of democratic countries worldwide, 1810–2010:
1810: 1 (small green)
1820: 1 (small blue)
1830: 1 (small orange)
1840: 1 (small light blue)
1850: 3 (small red)
1860: 4 (small dark blue)
1870: 5 (small salmon)
1880: 8 (light blue)
1890: 8 (blue)
1900: 10 (yellow)
1910: 12 (light salmon)
1920: 18 (blue-green)
1930: 15 (gray-blue)
1940: 11 (small pink)
1950: 29 (medium red)

1960: 30 (medium yellow)
1970: 29 (medium blue-green)
1980: 34 (medium salmon)
1990: 45 (medium light salmon)
2000: 70 (large light green)
2010: 89 (large light blue)

Source: Bastian Herre and Max Roser, "Democracy," *Our World in Data*, 2013, www.ourworldindata.org/democracy.

PAGES 24–25
DEMOCRACY II
17 ½ × 35 ¾ in. (44 × 91 cm)
Number of democracies vs. autocracies worldwide, 1920 vs. 2020:

1920 (left): 18 democracies vs. 132 autocracies
2020 (right): 99 democracies vs. 80 autocracies

Source: Bastien Herre and Max Roser, "Democracy," *Our World in Data*, 2013.

PAGE 28
STAYING ALIVE
25 ½ × 18 ⅞ in. (65 × 48 cm)
Life expectancy in Austria, the United States, and the United Kingdom over various periods of time, pending when data was available, 1550–2014 (top to bottom):

Austria, 1880–2014 (oval):
1880–1900: 30–40 years
1901–1920: 40–50 years
1921–1945: 50–60 years
1946–1964: 60–70 years
1965–2006: 70–80 years
2007–2014: 80–90 years

United States, 1880–2014 (horizontal rectangle):
1880–1901: 40–50 years
1902–1930: 50–60 years
1931–1960: 60–70 years
1961–2014: 70–80 years

United Kingdom, 1550–2014 (vertical rectangle):
1550–1558: 20–30 years
1559–1803: 30–40 years
1804–1902: 40–50 years
1903–1931: 50–60 years
1932–1953: 60–70 years
1954–2008: 70–80 years
2009–2014: 80–90 years

Sources: James C. Riley, "Estimates of Regional and Global Life Expectancy, 1800–2001," *Population Development Review* 31, no. 3 (2005): 537–43; Richard Zijdeman, "Life Expectancy at Birth," *Clio Infra*, 2012; UN Population Division, "World Population," *United Nations*, 2019.

PAGE 32
SPIKES
25 ¼ × 21 ¼ in. (64 × 54 cm)
Percentage of children vaccinated against diphtheria, whooping cough, and tetanus, 1880–2020 (clockwise from top):

1880: 0%   1960: 0%
1900: 0%   1980: 20%
1920: 0%   2000: 72%
1940: 0%   2020: 86%

Source: "Immunization and Vaccine-Preventable Communicable Diseases," *World Health Organization*, www.who.int/data/gho/data/themes/immunization. Note: Global data is available from 1980 to 2017. The vaccination rate refers to children (ages 12–23 months), not to the entire population.

PAGE 35
STARA BIEDA
15 ½ × 11 ½ in. (39 × 29 cm)
Worldwide poverty rate, 1920–2020:

1920: 70% (bottom)
1970: 48% (top)
2020: 9% (center)

Sources: François Bourguignon and Christian Morrisson, "Inequality Among World Citizens: 1820–1992," *American Economic Review* 92, no. 4 (2002): 727–44; Joe Hasell, Max Roser, Esteban Ortiz-Ospina and Pablo Arriagada, "Poverty," *Our World in Data*, 2022, www.ourworldindata.org/poverty.

PAGE 36
JOSEFINE
31 ½ × 25 ½ in. (80 × 65 cm)
Percentage of women working in the United States over one hundred years, 1910–2010 (top to bottom, left to right):

1910: 23%
1930: 24%
1950: 29%
1970: 43%
1990: 57%
2010: 59%

Source: Esteban Ortiz-Ospina, Sandra Tzvetkova, and Max Roser, "Women's Employment," *Our World in Data*, 2018, www.ourworldindata.org/female-labor-supply.

PAGE 39
JOHANNA
29 ½ × 24 ¾ in. (75 × 63 cm)
Global child mortality rate, 1800 vs. 2020:

1800: 43% (red)
2020: 3.9% (blue)

Source: Max Roser, Hannah Ritchie, and Bernadeta Dadonaite, "Child and Infant Mortality," *Our World in Data*, 2013, www.ourworldindata.org/child-mortality.

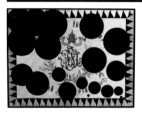

PAGES 40–41
WAR! WAR!
55 ⅛ × 70 in. (140 × 178 cm)
Percentage of years in which the great powers have fought one another for an extended period (at least twenty-five years), 1500–2000:

1500:	*75%*
1525:	*90%*
1550:	*100%*
1575:	*90%*
1600:	*75%*
1625:	*90%*
1650:	*100%*
1675:	*85%*
1700:	*80%*
1725:	*70%*
1750:	*40%*
1775:	*50%*
1800:	*60%*
1825:	*0%*
1850:	*25%*
1875:	*0%*
1900:	*20%*
1925:	*20%*
1950:	*10%*
1975:	*0%*
2000:	*0%*

Source: Steven Pinker, *The Better Angels of Our Nature*, New York, Viking: 2011.

PAGES 42 AND 43
DANGEROUS PEOPLE
Diptych, each panel: 24 ½ × 19 ¼ in. (62 × 49 cm)
Number of murders committed by female killers vs. male killers in the United States, 2020:
Page 42: *Murders committed by females*
13% (1,320)
Page 43: *Murders committed by males*
87% (8,977)

Source: "Arrest Trends by Gender, 2020," *Federal Bureau of Investigation*, 2021.

PAGES 46 AND 47
STUFF
60 × 45 ⅝ in. (152 × 116 cm)
Amount of stuff consumed yearly per person in the United Kingdom, 2000 vs. 2015:
Page 46, 2000: *15 tons*
Page 47, 2015: *10 tons*

Sources: Lynsey Brown, "UK Environmental Accounts: How Much Material Is the UK Consuming?" *Office for National Statistics*, 2016, www.ons.gov.uk/economy/environmental accounts/articles/ukenvironmentalaccountshowmuchmaterial istheukconsuming; Steven Pinker, *Enlightenment Now*, New York: Viking, 2018, 136.

PAGES 48–49
DOING/DUMPING
9 ½ × 12 ⅝ in. (24 × 32 cm)
Amount of greenhouse gases produced by the below activities, 2020:

Production (cement, steel, plastic):	*31%*
Electricity:	*25%*
Agriculture:	*19%*
Travel:	*16%*
Heating & cooling:	*7%*

Source: Bill Gates, *How to Avoid a Climate Disaster*, New York: Penguin Random House, 2021.

PAGES 50 AND 51
WATER
Diptych, each panel: 27 × 38 ½ in. (69 × 98 cm)
Share of world's population having water from a protected source, 1990–2015 (left to right):
Page 50:
1990: 75%   1998: 81%
Page 51:
2006: 86%   2015: 90%

Source: "Access to Drinking Water," *WHO/UNICEF Joint Monitoring Program for Water Supply and Sanitation*, 2022, www.data.unicef.org/topic/water-and-sanitation/drinking-water.

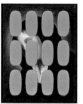

PAGE 52
SUICIDE I
20 ¼ × 16 in. (51 × 41 cm)
Yearly suicide rate in the United States per 100,000 people, 1950–2005 (top to bottom, left to right):
1950, 1955, 1960, 1965,
1970, 1975, 1980, 1985,
1990, 1995, 2000, 2005

Source: "Deaths by Suicide in the United States from 1950 to 2019, by Gender," *Statista*, 2022, www.statista.com/ statistics/187478/death-rate-from-suicide-in-the-us-by-gender-since-1950.

PAGE 55
DEMOCRACY I
21 ¼ × 21 ⅝ in. (54 × 55 cm)
Number of democracies worldwide, 1945–2015 (top to bottom):

1945:	*30*
1965:	*40*
1985:	*60*
2005:	*80*
2015:	*85*

Source: Bastien Herre and Max Roser, "Democracy," *Our World in Data*, 2013.

PAGE 56
FAMINE I
31 ½ × 27 ½ in. (80 × 70 cm)
Famine victims worldwide, 1860 vs. 2000:
1860: 4.1 million (yellow)
2000: 1.5 million (red)

Source: Joe Hasell and Max Roser, "Famines," *Our World in Data*, 2017, www.ourworldindata.org/famines.

PAGE 58

MOWING AND BLOWING

28 ⅜ × 23 ¼ in. (72 × 59 cm)

Amount of ozone-depleting pollution generated by leaf blowers vs. passenger cars, 2020

Source: "Small Engine Fact Sheet," *California Air Resources Board*, December 15, 2021, ww2.arb.ca.gov/resources/fact-sheets/sore-small-engine-fact-sheet.

PAGES 60–61

CARBON II

26 × 36 ½ in. (66 × 93 cm)

Carbon footprint of protein-rich foods per roughly two pounds (1 kg) of protein, 2018 (left to right):

Cheese: 187.4 lb (85 kg) CO_2
Chicken: 94.8 lb (43 kg) CO_2
Beef: 551.2 lb (250 kg) CO_2
Lamb: 441 lb (200 kg) CO_2
Farmed fish: 77.2 lb (35 kg) CO_2

Source: Hannah Ritchie, Pablo Rosado, and Max Roser, "Environmental Impacts of Food Production," *Our World in Data*, 2022, www.ourworldindata.org/environmental-impacts-of-food.

PAGES 64–65

FILTHY RICH

18 ⅞ × 51 in. (48 × 130 cm)

Percentage of global emissions by income class, 1990–2015:

Richest class (10%) are responsible for 52% of emissions (dark blue square);
Middle class (40%) are responsible for 41% of emissions (light blue circle);
Poorest class (50%) are responsible for 7% of emissions (black circle)

Source: Tim Gore, Mira Alestig, and Anna Ratcliff, "Confronting Carbon Inequality," *Oxfam International*, 2020, www.oxfam.org/en/press-releases/carbon-emissions-richest-1-percent-more-double-emissions-poorest-half-humanity.

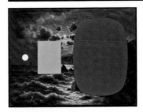

PAGE 68

CARBON I

29 ⅛ × 39 ⅜ in. (74 × 100 cm)

Cumulative emissions of CO_2 into the atmosphere, 1751–2015:
China (yellow circle)
United States (blue rectangle)
Europe (red oval)

Source: Hannah Ritchie, Pablo Rosado, and Max Roser, "Environmental Impacts of Food Production," *Our World in Data*, 2022.

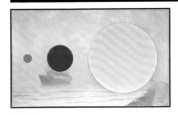

PAGE 69

OIL

23 ⅝ × 39 ⅜ in. (60 × 100 cm)

Number of large oil spills worldwide, 1975–2015:

1975: 115 (yellow)
1995:   23 (red)
2015:   6 (gray)

Source: "Oil Tanker Spill Statistics," *International Tanker Owners Pollution Federation*, 2022, www.itopf.org/knowledge-resources/data-statistics/statistics.

PAGES 70 AND 71

CORN/RICE/WHEAT

Diptych, each panel: 15 ⅜ × 12 ½ in. (39 × 32 cm)

Page 70:
Number of acres planted with grains, 1965 vs. 2005 (from the top):
1965: 650,000
2005: 650,000

Page 71:
Amount of global corn, rice, and wheat harvest in tons, 1965 vs. 2005 (from the top):
1965: 1,000,000
2005: 2,250,000

Source: Matt Ridley, *The Rational Optimist*, New York: HarperCollins, 2011, 121.

PAGE 72

MONEY TO LEARN

31 ½ × 24 ⅝ in. (80 × 63 cm)

Public education spending in developed nations as a percentage of GDP, 1880–2000 (top to bottom):

1880: 1.0% (green)
1900: 1.5% (orange)
1920: 1.8% (red)
1940: 2.0% (purple)
1960: 4.0% (red)
1980: 5.5% (dark red)
2000: 6.0% (yellow)

Source: Max Roser and Esteban Ortiz-Ospina, "Education Spending," *Our World in Data*, 2016, www.ourworldindata.org/financing-education.

PAGES 76 AND 77 (SHIRT)

BABIES

16 ½ × 13 ⅜ in. (42 × 34 cm)

Women in the United States dying in childbirth per 100,000 pregnant women, 1915 vs. 2015:

1915: 608 (purple)
2015:   14 (light blue)

Sources: Max Roser and Hannah Ritchie, "Maternal Mortality," *Our World in Data*, 2013, www.ourworldindata.org/maternal-mortality; Claudia Hanson, "Data on Maternal Mortality," Stockholm: Gapminder Foundation, 2010.

PAGES 80 (COAT), 81, AND BACK COVER

IN THE KITCHEN

26 ⅜ × 18 ½ in. (67 × 47 cm)

Percentage of people in the United States who believe that women should return to their traditional roles in society, 1990–2010:

2010:   *28%   (red)*
2000:   *34%   (blue)*
1990:   *49%   (yellow)*

Source: Pew Research Center, "Public Views on Changing Gender Roles," *Breadwinner Moms*, 6–12. Washington, DC: Pew Research Center, 2012, www.pewresearch.org/social-trends/2013/05/29/chapter-2-public-views-on-changing-gender-roles.

PAGE 83

HOT AND COLD

23 ¼ × 19 ⅝ in. (59 × 50 cm)

Percentage of households in the United States with running water, 1900–2000 (top to bottom):

1900:   *20%*
1950:   *80%*
2000:   *100%*

Source: Jeremy Greenwood, Ananth Seshadri, and Mehmet Yorukoglu, "Engines of Liberation," *The Review of Economic Studies* 72, no. 1 (2005): 109–33.

PAGES 84 AND 85

DIVISIONS

Diptych, each panel 19 ⅝ × 29 ½ in. (50 × 75 cm)

Page 84:
Agricultural usage of habitable land worldwide, 2020: 50%

Page 85 (left to right):
77% of agricultural land is used for meat and dairy, 23% is used for plants;

37% of daily protein supply comes from meat and dairy, 63% from plants;
18% of daily calorie supply comes from meat and dairy, 82% from plants

Source: "Land Use in Agriculture by the Numbers," *Food and Agriculture Organization of the United Nations*, May 7, 2020, www.fao.org/sustainability/news/detail/en/c/1274219.

PAGES 90 AND 93

CRIMINALS

Diptych, each panel: 27 ½ × 24 in. (70 × 61 cm)

Breakdown of different crimes committed by male vs. female perpetrators in the United States, 2011:

Page 90:
Murder: 87% male, 13% female (beige square)
Robbery: 88% male, 12% female (coral circle)
Burglary: 85% male, 15% female (blue-yellow circle)
Arson: 83% male, 17% female (blue-white rectangle)
Vandalism: 82% male, 18% female (purple-pink line)

Page 93:
Car theft: 82% male, 18% female (pink-white square)
Aggravated assault: 78% male, 22% female (green-pink circle)
Larceny theft: 57% male, 43% female (yellow-orange rectangle)
Embezzlement: 52% male, 48% female (purple-blue line)

Source: "Arrest Trends by Gender, 2011," *Federal Bureau of Investigation*, 2012.

PAGE 94

ROSALIA

24 × 19 ⅝ in. (61 × 50 cm)

Percentage of children around the world dying before reaching the age of five, 1870–2020:

1870:   40% (yellow)

1900:   36% (orange)
1930:   28% (red)
1960:   18% (blue)
1990:   9% (green)
2020:   4% (purple)

Sources: "Child Mortality Rate, Under Age Five," Stockholm: Gapminder Foundation, 2020; "Child Mortality and Causes of Death," *World Health Organization*, 2022, www.who.int/data/gho/data/themes/topics/sdg-target-3_2-newborn-and-child-mortality.

PAGE 95

READING AND WRITING

10 ⅝ × 8 ¼ in. (27 × 21 cm)

Number of children receiving an education worldwide, per one hundred children, 1820 vs. 2020:

1820:   17   (red)
2020:   86   (black)

Source: Max Roser and Esteban Ortiz-Ospina, "Primary and Secondary Education," *Our World in Data*, 2013, www.ourworldindata.org/primary-and-secondary-education.

PAGE 98 (DETAIL) AND 101

MS. MP

58 ⅝ × 41 in. (149 × 104 cm)

Percentage of parliamentary governments around the world which have voted in their first female representative, 1920–2020 (top to bottom):

1920:   15%
1940:   27%
1960:   61%
1980:   82%
2000:   94%
2020:   97%

Source: "Proportion of Seats Held by Women in National Parliaments," *Our World in Data*, 2022.

PAGE 102
HER MONEY
29 ½ × 23 ½ in. (75 × 60 cm)

Share of women in the United Kingdom in the top 10 percent of income earners, 1995–2015:

1995: 20% (rectangle, left)
2000: 22% (circle, top)
2005: 25% (circle, center)
2010: 28% (circle, bottom)
2015: 28% (rectangle, right)

Source: Anthony Atkinson, Alessandra Casarico, and Sarah Voitchovsky, "Top Incomes and the Gender Divide," *Journal of Economic Inequality* 16, no. 2, (2018): 225–56.

PAGES 104–5
THIRTY-SEVEN
15 ⅜ × 19 ¼ in. (39 × 49 cm)

Hours spent at work per week in the United States, 1900 vs. 2000:

1900: 55 hours (black)
2000: 37 hours (white)

Source: Valerie Ramey and Neville Francis, "A Century of Work and Leisure," *American Economic Journal: Macroeconomics* 1, no. 2 (2009): 189–224.

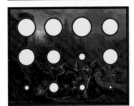

PAGES 108 (DETAIL) AND 111
WAR!
17 ⅜ × 22 in. (44 × 56 cm)

Percentage of years in which the great powers have fought one another for an extended period (at least twenty-five years), 1543–2016 (left to right, top to bottom):

1543: 95%
1586: 95%

1629: 100%
1672: 90%
1715: 85%
1758: 38%
1801: 62%
1844: 20%
1887: 10%
1930: 20%
1973: 15%
2016: 0%

Source: Steven Pinker, *The Better Angels of Our Nature*, New York, Viking: 2011.

PAGE 112
A SMALL WORLD
35 ¾ × 28 ¾ in. (91 × 73 cm)

Number of visitors to the five most popular museums in New York, 2018:
Metropolitan Museum of Art:
   6.9 million (black)
American Museum of Natural History:
   4.9 million (purple)
9/11 Memorial Museum:
   3.1 million (yellow)
Museum of Modern Art:
   2.7 million (green)
Whitney Museum:
   1 million (pink)

Sources: Emily Sharpe, José da Silva, Valentina Bin, Anna Musini, and Vanessa Thill, "Art's Most Popular: Most Visited Shows and Museums 2018," *Art Newspaper*, April 2019; "A Year in Review: 2018," *National September 11 Memorial & Museum*, www.reports.911memorial.org/2018-report.

PAGES 114 AND 117 (DETAIL)
SCRIPTURES
29 ⅛ × 24 ½ in. (74 × 62 cm)

Number of books published per one million people in the United Kingdom, 1600–2000:

1600:   65 (white star)
1800:   298 (green star)
2000: 1,745 (purple triangle)

Source: Jonathan Fink-Jensen, "Book Titles Per Capita," *Cilo Infra*, 2015.

PAGE 126
TWO MARKETS
Cotton T-shirt

Global art market sales vs. global sales of diapers, 2020:
Art: $50.1 billion (white)
Diapers: $50.7 billion (black)

Sources: "Global Art Market Value," *Statista*, March 2022, www.statista.com/statistics/883755/global-art-market-value; "Adule and Baby Diapers Global Market Value," *Statista*, July 2022, www.statista.com/statistics/1325252/adult-and-baby-diapers-global-market-value.
CG-generated artwork: Santiago Carrasquilla, Art Camp

PAGES 144–45
TWO MARKETS
26 ¾ × 38 in. (68 × 97 cm)

Global art market sales vs. global sales of diapers, 2020:
Art: $50.1 billion (black)
Diapers: $50.7 billion (red)

Sources: "Global Art Market Value," *Statista*, March 2022; "Adule and Baby Diapers Global Market Value," *Statista*, July 2022.

PAGES 148–49
BEING SOCIAL
35 ½ × 54 ¾ in. (90 × 139 cm)

Percentage of GDP spent on social programs in the United States, 1920–2020:

1920:   1% of GDP (blue line)
1955:   5% of GDP (yellow circle)
1980: 15% of GDP (green circle)
2020: 20% of GDP (purple line)

Source: Esteban Ortiz-Ospina and Max Roser, "Government Spending," *Our World in Data*, 2016, www.ourworldindata.org/government-spending.

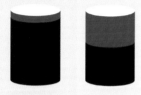

PAGES 152 AND 155

INEQUALITY

60 × 46 in. (152 × 117 cm)

Income inequality in the United States, according to the Gini Index (0–1), 1900–2000 (showing 1900 and 1966, respectively):

1900: 0.47   *1966: 0.35*
1933: 0.42   *2000: 0.42*

Source: Branko Milanovic, *Global Inequality: A New Approach for the Age of Globalization*, Cambridge, MA: Harvard University, 2016.

PAGE 156

WORKING A JOB

60 × 46 in. (152 × 117 cm)

Hours spent at work per week in Europe and the United States combined, 1900–2000 (showing 1900):

1900: 61 hours
1933: 45 hours
1966: 40 hours
2000: 43 hours

Source: Charlie Giattino, Esteban Ortiz-Ospina, and Max Roser, "Working Hours," *Our World in Data*, 2020, www.ourworldindata.org/working-hours.

PAGES 158 AND 159

WORKING AT HOME

Diptych, each panel: 60 × 46 in. (152 × 117 cm)

Hours spent on household work per week worldwide, 2020 vs. 1900:
Page 158, 2020: *22 hours*
Page 159, 1900: *58 hours*

Source: Rob Wijnberg, "The Great Paradox of Our Time: Everything Is Both Better and Worse Than Ever Before," *The Correspondent*, 2019, www.thecorrespondent.com/104/ the-great-paradox-of-our-time-everything-is-both-better- and-worse-than-ever-before.

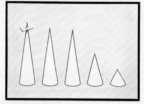

PAGE 162 (DETAIL)

ILLITERACY

Embroidery on cotton, 54 ¾ × 77 ½ in. (139 × 197 cm)

Percentage of the world's population that is illiterate, 1820–2020 (left to right):

1820: 85%
1870: 81%
1920: 78%
1970: 49%
2020: 18%

Source: Max Roser and Esteban Ortiz-Ospina, "Literacy," *Our World in Data*, 2016.
Created in collaboration with Yau Jiang Ping, Su Embroidery, China.

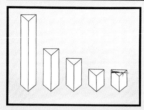

PAGES 166–67

HOMICIDE

Embroidery on cotton, 54 ¾ × 77 ½ in. (139 × 197 cm)

Number of murders in Italy per 100,000 people, 1820–2020 (left to right):

1820: 17
1870: 9
1920: 4
1970: 2
2020: 1

Source: Manuel Eisner, "Long-Term Historical Trends in Violent Crime," *Crime and Justice* 30 (2003): 83–142. Created in collaboration with Yau Jiang Ping, Su Embroidery, China.

PAGES 178 AND 181

MURDEROUS COAT

Tapestry fabric created in France, coat made in New York

Number of homicides in Europe per 100,000 people, 1400–2000 (top to bottom):

1400: 35
1450: 30
1500: 25
1550: 23
1600: 20
1650: 18
1700: 16
1750: 8
1800: 3
1850: 3
1900: 2.5
1950: 2
2000: 2

Source: Manuel Eisner, "Long-Term Historical Trends in Violent Crime," 83–142.
Photo: Henry Hargreaves

PAGES 182, 183, AND 185 (DETAIL)

OPINION COAT

Cotton twill from Japan, coat made in New York

Percentage of people in the United States who believe that women should return to their traditional roles in society, 1910–2010:

2010: 28% (red)
2000: 34% (blue)
1990: 49% (yellow)

Source: Pew Research Center, "Public Views on Changing Gender Roles," 6–12.
Photo: Henry Hargreaves

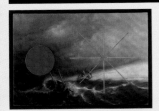

PAGE 186

QUAKES, FLOODS, HURRICANES

15 × 22 ½ in. (38 × 57 cm)

Number of deaths worldwide as a result of natural disasters, 1920–1930 vs. 2010–2020:

1920–1930: 525,000 (red circle)
2010–2020: 60,000 (star shape)

Source: Hannah Ritchie and Max Roser, "Natural Disasters," *Our World in Data*, 2021, www.ourworldindata.org/natural-disasters.

PAGE 187

QUAKES, FLOODS, HURRICANES

Cotton long-sleeved shirt

Number of deaths worldwide as a result of natural disasters, 1920–1930 vs. 2010–2020:

1920–1930: 525,000 (red circle)
2010–2020: 60,000 (star shape)

Source: Hannah Ritchie and Max Roser, "Natural Disasters," *Our World in Data*, 2021.
Photo: Henry Hargreaves

PAGE 188

LIFE

Japanese cotton shirt with cotton inserts

Average global life expectancy, 1800 vs. 2020 (top to bottom):

1800: 29 years
2020: 71 years

Source: Max Roser, Esteban Ortiz-Ospina, and Hannah Ritchie, "Life Expectancy," *Our World in Data*, 2013, www.ourworldindata.org/lifeexpectancy.
Photo: Henry Hargreaves

PAGE 189

LIFE

22 ¼ × 18 ¼ in. (57 × 46 cm)

Average global life expectancy, 1800 vs. 2020 (top to bottom):

1800: 29 years
2020: 71 years

Source: Max Roser, Esteban Ortiz-Ospina, and Hannah Ritchie, "Life Expectancy," *Our World in Data*, 2013.

PAGE 192

THIS SUM AIN'T ZERO

26 ¾ × 38 ½ in. (68 × 98 cm)

Trade Openness Index (the sum of all world exports and imports, as a share of the world's GDP), 1917 vs. 2017:

1917: 10% (light blue rectangle)
2017: 50% (purple ring)

Sources: Mariko Klasing and Petros Milionis, "Quantifying the Evolution of World Trade, 1870–1949," *Journal of International Economics* 92, no. 1 (2014): 185–97; Esteban Ortiz-Ospina, Diana Beltekian, and Max Roser, "Trade and Globalization," *Our World in Data*, 2018, www.ourworldindata.org/trade-and-globalization.

PAGES 196–97

SUICIDE II

27 ¼ × 43 in. (69 × 109 cm)

Yearly suicide rate worldwide per 100,000 people, 2000 vs. 2015:

2000: 13 (black)
2015: 11 (white)

Source: "Deaths by Suicide in the United States from 1950 to 2019, by Gender," *Statista*, 2022.

PAGE 198

Lobmeyr glassware, 2022
(top to bottom, left to right):

HEALTH & SICKNESS

Percentage of Europe's GDP spent on health care, 1820 vs. 2020 (from the top):

1820: 0%
2020: 9%

Source: Peter Lindert, "Social Spending and the Welfare State," *How Was Life? New Perspectives on Well-being and Global Inequality since 1820*, Paris: Organization for Economic Co-operation and Development, 2014.

LIFE & DEATH

Worldwide life expectancy, 1820 vs. 2019 (from the top):

1820: 29 years
2019: 73 years

Source: Max Roser, Esteban Ortiz-Ospina, and Hannah Ritchie, "Life Expectancy," *Our World in Data*, 2013.

KNOWLEDGE & IGNORANCE

Percentage of global population that can read and write, 1820–2016 (from the top):

1820: 12%
1918: 28%
2016: 82%

Source: Max Roser and Esteban Ortiz-Ospina, "Literacy," *Our World in Data*, 2016.

DEMOCRACY & DICTATORSHIP

Number of democratic countries worldwide, 1820–2016 (from the top):

1820: 12
1885: 19
1951: 58
2016: 82

Source: Bastian Herre and Max Roser, "Democracy," *Our World in Data*, 2013.

FOOD & HUNGER

Percentage of the world population having escaped extreme poverty, 1820–2015 (from the top):

1820: 16%
1870: 25%
1920: 40%
1970: 64%
2015: 90%

Source: Joe Hasell, Max Roser, Esteban Ortiz-Ospina and Pablo Arriagada, "Poverty," *Our World in Data*, 2022.

PEACE & WAR

Percentage of years in which the great powers did not fight one another, over twenty-five-year periods, 1795–2015 (from the top):

1795–1820: 35%
1835–860: 75%
1875–1900: 90%
1915–1940: 60%
1955–1980: 90%
1990–2015: 100%

Source: Jack Levy and William Thompson, *Causes of War*, Malden: Wiley-Blackwell, 2011.
Photo: © Klaus Fritsch for Lobmeyr

PAGES 206–7
Lobmeyr glassware, 2021
(left to right):

Percentage of marine protected areas around the world, 2016 vs. 2017 (from the top):
2016: 9%
2017: 11.5%

Source: "Increased Growth of Protected Areas in 2017," *Protected Planet*, 2017, www.protectedplanet.net/en/news-and-stories/increased-growth-of-protected-areas-in-2017.

Number of countries who signed the Paris Agreement of the UN Climate Change Convention, 2000–2015 (left to right):

2000: 184
2003: 187
2006: 188
2009: 193
2012: 195
2015: 197

Source: "The Paris Agreement," *United Nations*, www.un.org/en/climatechange/paris-agreement.

Monetary pledges to the Green Climate Fund, various countries, 2018 (clockwise from top left):

Sweden: $0.5 billion
United States: $3.0 billion
United Kingdom: $1.2 billion
France: $1.0 billion
Germany: $1.0 billion
Norway: $0.25 billion
Switzerland: $0.1 billion
Austria: $0.03 billion

Source: "Initial Resource Mobilization," *Green Climate Fund*, 2021, www.greenclimate.fund/about/resource-mobilisation.

Amount of stuff consumed yearly per average person in the United Kingdom, 2001 vs. 2013 (from the top):

2001: 15 tons
2013: 10 tons

Source: Steven Pinker, *Enlightenment Now*, 136.

Percentage of important global biodiversity sites that are environmentally protected, 2000–2018 (clockwise from left):

2000: 33%
2009: 43%
2018: 45%

Source: Hannah Ritchie, Fiona Spooner, and Max Roser, "Biodiversity," *Our World in Data*, 2022, www.ourworldindata.org/biodiversity.

Percentage of world population without access to clean water, 1990–2015 (from the top):

1990: 25%
1995: 21%
2000: 18%
2005: 15%
2010: 12%
2015: 9%

Source: "Access to Drinking Water," *WHO/UNICEF Joint Monitoring Program for Water Supply and Sanitation*, 2022, www.data.unicef.org/topic/water-and-sanitation/drinking-water.
Illustrations: Raxenne Maniquiz
Photo: © Atelier Courbet

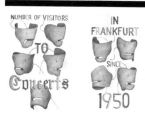

PAGES 216 AND 218 (DETAILS)
Hand-painted mural, Flemings Hotel, Frankfurt, Germany

Number of visitors to concerts in Frankfurt since 1950:

1950: 317,000
1955: 830,000
1960: 835,000
1965: 1,019,000
1970: 900,000
1975: 765,000
1980: 695,000
1985: 695,000
1990: 1,252,000
1995: 1,009,000
2000: 1,143,000
2005: 960,000
2010: 1,057,000
2015: 1,154,000

Source: Statistics annual, *Frankfurt am Main*.
Illustration: Jason Holley
Photo: © Flemings Hotel

PAGES 219, 220–21 (DETAILS)
Hand-painted mural, Flemings Hotel, Frankfurt, Germany

Number of ice cream parlors in Frankfurt since 1950 (detail, left to right):

1960: 10
1970: 16
1980: 23

Source: Address books (1950–2015), *Frankfurt am Main*.
Illustration: Jason Holley
Photo: © Flemings Hotel

PAGE 222
EVE
20 × 15 in. (51 × 38 cm)
Collective harvest of the world's apples, 1962–2017 (top to bottom):
1962:   22 million
1973:   29 million
1984:   40 million
1995:   49 million
2006:   63 million
2017:   83 million

Source: "Apple Production," *Food and Agriculture Organization of the United Nations*, 2022.

PAGE 227
ACCIDENTS
24 ½ × 16 ⅛ in. (62 × 41 cm)
Yearly fatal occupational accidents in the United States per 100,000 workers, 1910–2010:
1910:   63   (light green shape)
1960:   28   (yellow circle)
2010:   5   (white line)

Source: Steven Pinker, *Enlightenment Now*, 187.
Note: Data is from different sources and may not be completely commensurable.

PAGES 234–35
PRECEDENTS
15 × 26 ⅜ in. (38 × 67 cm)
Deaths as a result of global pandemics over the past 200 years (left to right):
Spanish flu (1918–1919):   *45 million*
HIV/AIDS (1981–present):   *30 million*
Third Plague (1855):   *12 million*
COVID-19 (2019–present):   *4 million*

Sources: "History of 1918 Flu Pandemic," *Centers for Disease Control and Prevention*, March 21, 2018, www.cdc.gov/flu/pandemic-resources/1918-commemoration/1918-pandemic-history; Nicholas LePan and Harrison Schell, "Visualizing the History of Pandemics," *Visual Capitalist*, March 6, 2023, www.visualcapitalist.com/history-of-pandemics-deadliest.

PAGE 226
HIGH AND LOW
25 ½ × 21 ⅝ in. (65 × 55 cm)
Average life expectancy at birth in the United Kingdom, 1700 vs. 2020:
1700:   37 years   (purple)
2020:   75 years   (light blue)

Sources: Max Roser, Esteban Ortiz-Ospina, and Hannah Ritchie, "Life Expectancy," *Our World in Data*, 2013; Richard Zijdeman, "Life Expectancy at Birth," *Cilo Infra*, 2012; "England & Wales Civilian Population," *Human Mortality Database*, n.d.

PAGE 231
ESSERE SOCIALE
20 ½ × 13 ½ in. (52 × 34 cm)
Percentage of GDP spent on social programs in Italy, 1930–2010:
1930:   1%   (blue line)
1970:   14%   (blue rectangle)
2010:   26%   (beige shape)

Source: Max Roser and Esteban Ortiz-Ospina, "Government Spending," *Our World in Data*, 2016.

SELECTED SOLO EXHIBTIONS

2001
Stefan Sagmeister, Gallery Frédéric Sanchez, Paris

2002
Handarbeit, Museum of Applied Arts, Vienna

2003
Handarbeit, Museum für Gestaltung, Zurich
Stefan Sagmeister, GGG Gallery, Tokyo
Stefan Sagmeister, DDD Gallery, Osaka

2004
Stefan Sagmeister, Zeroone Design Center, Seoul

2007
Low Expectations Are a Good Strategy, Wolfsonian,
  Miami, FL
Things I Have Learned In My Life So Far, Galerija Ava,
  Ljubljana, Slovenia

2008
Things I Have Learned In My Life So Far, Deitch Projects,
  New York
Things I Have Learned In My Life So Far, around Brno,
  Czech Republic

2011
*Sagmeister, Another Show about Promotion and Advertising
  Material*, Mudac, Lausanne, Switzerland
*Sagmeister, Another Show about Promotion and Advertising
  Material*, Musée des Arts Décoratifs, Paris

2012
*Sagmeister, Another Show about Promotion and Advertising
  Material*, Museum of the Image, Breda, Netherlands
The Happy Show, Institute of Contemporary Art,
  Philadelphia
Sagmeister Inc., Hanbit Media Park, Seoul

2013
The Happy Show, Design Exchange, Toronto
The Happy Show, MOCA, Pacific Design Center,
  Los Angeles
Six Things: Sagmeister & Walsh, Jewish Museum,
  New York
The Happy Show, Chicago Cultural Center,
  Chicago
Sagmeister Inc, Imam Ali Museum, Tehran, Iran
The Happy Show, Gaite Lyrique, Paris

2015
The Happy Show, Museum of Applied Arts,
  Vienna
The Happy Show, Museum of Vancouver,
  Vancouver
The Happy Show, Museum für angewandte Kunst,
  Frankfurt

2017
Designer Selects, Museum für Gestaltung, Zurich

2018
The Happy Show, Museum of Art, Architecture and
  Technology, Lisbon

2018
Sagmeister & Walsh: Beauty, Museum of Applied Arts,
  Vienna

2019
Sagmeister & Walsh: Beauty, Museum Angewandte Kunst,
  Frankfurt
Sagmeister & Walsh: Beauty, Museum für Kunst und
  Gewerbe, Hamburg

2021
Sagmeister & Walsh: Beauty, Fondation d'Entreprise Martell,
  Cognac, France
Beautiful Numbers, Thomas Erben Gallery, New York

2022
Sagmeister & Walsh: Beauty, Vorarlberg Museum, Bregenz,
  Austria
Belleza en Cifras (Beautiful Numbers), Museo Franz Mayer,
  Mexico City

2023
Now Is Better, Patrick Parrish Gallery, New York
Belleza en Cifras, University of Monterrey, Mexico
Gorgeous Numbers, DDD Gallery, Tokyo

SELECTED GROUP EXHIBITIONS

2000
Design Biannual, Cooper-Hewitt National Design
  Museum, New York

2001
Stealing Eyeballs, Kuenstlerhaus, Vienna

2007
Biennale Jogja, Jakarta, Indonesia

2008
Rough Cut, Museum of Modern Art, New York

2010
Curious Minds, Israel Museum, Jerusalem

2011
Austria Davaj!, Schusev State Museum of Architecture,
  Moscow
Bewegte Schrift, Museum für Gestaltung, Zurich
Standard Deviations, Museum of Modern Art, New York

2014

Vorbilder, Museum of Applied Arts, Vienna

2016

New Creatures, OCT Art & Design Gallery, Shenzhen, China

2018

Beauty = Function, Biennale de Venezia, Austrian Pavillion, Venice

2022

Seeing Red, Looking Blue, Feeling Green, Marquee Projects, Bellport, NY
First Stone, National Coach Museum, Lisbon

RESIDENCIES

2014

Designer in Residence, German Academy, Villa Massimo, Rome

2016

Designer in Residence, Exploratorium, San Francisco

2019

Designer in Residence, American Academy, Rome

SELECTED BIBLIOGRAPHY

Stefan Sagmeister and Peter Hall, *Made You Look*, London: Booth-Clibborn, 2001

Stefan Sagmeister, *Things I Have Learned In My Life So Far*, New York: Abrams, 2008

Stefan Sagmeister, *Another Book about Promotion & Sales Material*, New York: Abrams, 2011

Stefan Sagmeister and Jessica Walsh, *Beauty*, New York: Phaidon, 2018

ACKNOWLEDGMENTS

I would like to thank the wonderful Philipp Hubert for designing this book with me. Thank you so much for your expertise and never-ending patience.

The text was improved steadily by Phaidon editor Stephanie Holstein and the terrific Deborah Aaronson, who never tired of correcting our sloppy thinking and terrible grammar. Rachel Walther expertly copyedited the text, and Lindsey Westbrook diligently proofread it. Thanks, too, to photo researcher Liz Grady.

Thank you, Bertram Schmidt-Friderichs of Verlag Hermann Schmidt, the publisher of the book's German edition, who organized a first-rate translation of the manuscript.

We are also grateful to all the people who organized my lectures on long-term thinking around the world. These talks allowed me to try out different themes and bring a degree of focus to this vast subject.

Thank you to all the fantastic galleries and museums that have allowed us to show this work in their spaces and share this content with the world, including the Thomas Erben Gallery and the Patrick Parrish Gallery, both in New York; and the Museo Franz Mayer, Mexico City, Udem, Monterrey, and Museo Arocena in Torreón, all in Mexico. Additional thanks to everybody at the GGG Gallery in Tokyo.

Thank you to the phenomenal team at the Brooklyn Navy Yard (and beyond) who helped create the inserts for the historical canvases, including Ting Yih, Tine Kindermann, Roman Erlikh, Robert Kalka, Alex Whyte, Eric Porter, Kevin Shade, and Bill Delaney.

Carlo Ferraris at Allegheny Productions did a wonderful job with the framing. Thank you to Chris Dean at Parallax Printing for the incredibly exact translation of my files into large lenticulars with very little ghosting.

Thank you to Anni Kuan for the managing the detailed production of the clothes, and to Santiago Carrasquilla for excellent videos of the clothes and corresponding artworks.

I also would like to thank my sisters—Andrea, Christine, and Veronika—and my brothers, Gebhard and Martin, for their tremendous support and for giving me, despite having lived in New York for almost thirty years, the feeling that I am still properly rooted in Austria too.

And most of all, I'd love to thank my partner, Karolina Ciecholewska, for always helping with many decisions, large and small. You are the light.

Phaidon Press Limited
2 Cooperage Yard
London E15 2QR

Phaidon Press Inc.
65 Bleecker Street
New York, New York 10012

phaidon.com

First published 2023
© 2023 Phaidon Press Limited

ISBN 978 1 8386 6696 5
ISBN 978 1 8386 6761 0 (Signed Edition)

A CIP catalogue record for this book is available from the British Library
and the Library of Congress.

Design
Stefan Sagmeister and Philipp Hubert

Photography
Historical paintings: Philip Reed and Andreas Vesterlund
Clothes: Henry Hargreaves

Headline Typography
Saad Moosajee

Editors
Stephanie Holstein and Deborah Aaronson

Production
Adela Cory

Image Licensing
Liz Grady

Typefaces
Replica (Lineto), Sectra (Grilli Type), Beatrice (Sharp Type), DIN (Linotype)

Lenticular Print
Design: Matteo Pani, Emily Roemer

Historical Paintings
Ting Yih, Tine Kindermann, Roman Erlikh, Robert Kalka,
Alex Whyte, Eric Porter, Kevin Shade, Bill Delaney

Embroideries
Suzhou Yao-Jian

Illustrations
The Ledger, Bentonville, and Lobmeyr Glasses by Raxenne Maniquiz
Flemings Hotel, Frankfurt, by Jason Holley
The Tunnels in Toronto by Linus Lohoff
3D images of clothes by Santiago Carrasquilla, Art Camp

Printed in China

Image Credits
Robert Alexander/Getty Images: 135. © 2022 The Andy Warhol Foundation for
the Visual Arts, Inc./Licensed by Artists Rights Society (ARS), New York: 128
(far left). Artefact/Alamy Stock Photo: 134 (left). © Atelier Courbet: 204–207.
Hans-Joerg Bergler: 120. Bela Borsodi: 140. DB Burkeman: 124. Santiago
Carrasquilla/Artcamp: 126, 182-183, 187, 201. Matthias Ernstberger: 139.
© Flemings Hotel, Frankfurt: 219. Henry Hargreaves: 77, 80, 178, 181, 185, 188, back
cover flap. © Mona Heiss: 170 (third row). © Lobmeyr: 198. © ICA Philadelphia:
170 (first row, right). © Illy, Illy Art Collection: 200, 202–203. © The Ledger,
Bentonville, AR: 208, 212–215. Linus Lohoff and Nigel Scott: 239. © MAK/Aslan
Kudrnofsky: 170 (first row, left; second row, bottom row). Raxenne Maniquiz: 210.
© Mayer of Munich: 211. © MDA Singapore: 141. Giorgio Morara, stock.adobe.
com: 131 left. © Move Our Money: 248, 250, 251. © Museo Franz Mayer, Mexico
City: 176–177. © Ressence: 190, 193, 194. © Martin Sagmeister: 54, 57. Christine
Schneider Sagmeister: 119. Nigel Scott: 238. © Simon Tanenbaum: 240, 241,
244, 245, 246–247. Daniele da Volterra: 131 right. Andreas Vesterlund: 160–161,
168–169, 172–173, 174–175. VM/BL/Alamy Stock Photo: 134 (right). wowinside,
stock.adobe.com: 131 (center). Ting Yih: 88, 89, 122–123.